Twayne's United States Authors Series

Sylvia E. Bowman, *Editor*

INDIANA UNIVERSITY

Ida M. Tarbell

 247

Ida M. Tarbell

IDA M. TARBELL

By MARY E. TOMKINS

Michigan State University

Twayne Publishers, Inc. :: New York

Library of Congress Cataloging in Publication Data

Tomkins, Mary E.
    Ida M. Tarbell.

    (Twayne's United States authors series, TUSAS 247)
    Bibliography: p. 171.
    1. Tarbell, Ida Minerva, 1857–1944.
PS3539.A58Z9   070.9'24   73-22293
ISBN 0-8057-0714-X

To Monica, David, and James

Contents

About the Author

Mary E. Tomkins left her home town, Philadelphia, Pennsylvania, soon after completing high school. At one time or another since then she has lived in all sections of the United States and calls all of them home. Reversing the usual process, she married and had three children before going to college. Between moves she attended community colleges in Los Angeles, California and Odessa, Texas. She completed her undergraduate work at the University of Utah in 1959. That year National Education Act fellowships became available for graduate students intending to become college teachers. Offered an NDEA fellowship, Professor Tomkins accepted. She remained at the University of Utah, pursuing an interdisciplinary program which led, in 1964, to a Ph. D. degree in English.

Thereafter, she taught English at Portland State University. In 1965 she joined the faculty of the Department of American Thought and Language at Michigan State University, where she is now a professor. She has published studies of the poetry of Walt Whitman and that of Stephen Vincent Benet. In addition, she has written papers on such varied figures in American intellectual life as John Dewey, Randolph Bourne, William Styron, and Margaret Fuller.

The present work results from the author's interest in the unique role of the muckrakers in articulating and channeling public outrage over commercial and political corruption so that it resulted in substantive reforms. Seldom have journalists had such opportunity to be agents of social change.

Preface

Mention of Ida Minerva Tarbell's name today among people who read books like this one elicits a predictable response: "She's the Muckraker who wrote about Standard Oil. Isn't she?" She was indeed that Muckraker; and her *History of the Standard Oil Company*, published in 1904, has imprinted her memory indelibly, if nowadays a bit dimly, on the American consciousness, where her book is recalled as the signal that put a stop to unregulated monopoly in the oil industry.

Although now regarded as a one-book author, Tarbell was, throughout her fifty-year career as a working journalist, a highly productive writer. The great bulk of her work first appeared in mass-circulation magazines whose development was greatly aided by her and her colleagues on the staff of *McClure's Magazine* around the turn of the century. The best of her work was collected, and I discuss mainly these books in this study. My plan is to place them in perspective relative to her *History of the Standard Oil Company* and to examine that great work in terms of its time, of Tarbell's career as a whole, and of her background which equipped her to write it.

This book, which was more than the result of the usual journalistic assignment, concerned an issue she had grown up with in the Oil Regions of Western Pennsylvania, where her father had been an independent oil operator since shortly after the discovery of oil there in 1859. The issue centered on the struggle between small, local, independent oil operators and a huge, impersonal, outside corporation for control of the nation's oil resources. Ultimately, the issue concerned, and continues to concern, the threat to traditional institutions represented by corporate capitalism. Because the issue is still vital and still unresolved, Tarbell's *History of the Standard Oil Company* continues to be relevant—if largely unread. Although the remainder of her work was topical, an examination of it reveals a unified view of her hopes for this country and illuminates also the hopes for social betterment of the Progressive era.

I have presented this study in chronological order and have attempted to show how significant events in Tarbell's life affected her work and help to explain it. The focus is held primarily upon her work. Her autobiography, *All in the Day's Work*, indicates by its very title how large a place work played in her life, and reading it reveals her joy in her chosen work, never gushy, but deep and steady.

For assistance in completion of various phases of this book I wish to thank Philip M. Benjamin, Librarian of the Reis Library at Allegheny College, Meadville, Pennsylvania, for permission to use the extensive collection of Ida Tarbell's papers held there. My particular thanks are gratefully extended to Dorothy J. Smith, Assistant Librarian of that library, for her many kindnesses and help with materials during my stay there. Thanks also to Alan W. Perkins, Curator of the holdings in the museum at Drake Well Park, Titusville, Pennsylvania, for permission to examine the Tarbell papers there. In addition my thanks are due to Marcia Williams Bradley, Director of the Sophia Smith Collection in the Smith College Library, Northampton, Massachusetts, and to Elizabeth S. Duvall, Bibliographer of the collection, for access to the Tarbell papers there. My gratitude is owed to Michigan State University for a research grant which aided completion of this study. Finally, I wish to express my profound appreciation of my three children's patience and encouragement during the course of this work.

MARY E. TOMKINS

East Lansing, Michigan

Chronology

1857   Ida Minerva Tarbell born on her pioneer grand-parents' farm, Erie County, Pennsylvania, November 5.

1860   Father enters oil business; moves family from farm to first home, on Cherry Run Creek, in a new Oil Region settlement soon to become city of Rouseville.

1870   Family moves to Titusville, Pennsylvania, where Ida receives regular schooling and completes high school.

1876   Enters Allegheny College, Meadville, Pennsylvania; majors in biology.

1880– Graduates from college; starts teaching at Poland
1882   Union Seminary, Poland, Ohio. Quits after two years of staggering teaching load and low pay; returns home.

1883   Receives master of arts degree at Allegheny College; joins editorial staff of *The Chautauquan;* learns magazine business thoroughly; becomes managing editor.

1886   First articles published in *The Chautauquan.*

1890   Quits *The Chautauquan;* goes to Paris to study historiography at the Sorbonne and the College de France. Does research on biography of French Revolutionary figure Madame Roland. Supports self by writing articles about Paris for American newspapers. Sale of short story to *Scribner's Magazine* buoys confidence in ability.

1893   Returns to United States to work for *McClure's Magazine*. First big assignment, a biography of Napoleon.

1894– Popularity of series on Napoleon (runs from November,
1895   1894, to April, 1895) ensures financial success of magazine; later publishes as *A Short Life of Napoleon Bonaparte*. Starts work on next assignment, a biography of Abraham Lindoln.

1896   Lincoln biography of early years completed in *McClure's*, in November. Published as *The Early Life of Abraham Lincoln*, with coauthor J. McCan Davis. *Madame Roland: A Biographical Study* published.

1897   As associate editor of *McClure's* works with S. S.
        McClure and a brilliant staff to make the magazine a
        best seller. Continues Lincoln biography.

1900   *The Life of Abraham Lincoln* published in two vol-
        umes. Begins research on a series about the rise of the
        Standard Oil Company.

1902–   *History of the Standard Oil Company*, accompanied
1904   by publication of articles on municipal corruption by
        Lincoln Steffens and corruption in labor unions by
        Ray Stannard Baker, inaugurates muckraking era.
        History of the Standard Oil Company published im-
        mediately after serialization.

1906   Policy differences split *McClure's* staff. John S. Phillips
        as editor in chief, Tarbell, Steffens, Baker, and Finley
        Peter Dunne purchase *The American Magazine* and
        compete against *McClure's*. Theodore Roosevelt
        denounces writers of exposés as "muckrakers." Tarbell
        works on new series to expose tariff abuses.

1907   Collection of Lincoln anecdotes published as *He Knew
        Lincoln*. First part of tariff series concluded in June.

1909   *Father Abraham*, Lincoln stories, published.

1910   Writes series on women; tariff series resumed.

1911   Series published as *The Tariff in Our Times*. Editor
        of *Selections from the Letters, Speeches, and State
        Papers of Abraham Lincoln*.

1912   Magazine series on women (from January through
        December) published as *The Business of Being a
        Woman*.

1914–   Serial in *The American* propagandizing for Frederick
1915   Taylor's scientific management methods in industry
        (appearing from October, 1914 to September, 1915)
        demonstrates Tarbell's shift from negative to positive
        attitude toward business goals. Series in *Woman's
        Home Companion* published as *Ways of Woman*.
        Career on *American Magazine* ends; becomes Chau-
        tauqua lecturer.

1916   *New Ideals in Business*.

1917   Involved in war effort; accepts appointment to Presi-
        dent Wilson's Women's Committee of the Council of
        National Defense. Serves throughout war.

1919   Member of President Wilson's Industrial Conference.

Joins *Red Cross Magazine* staff in Paris under John Phillips as editor. Covers Paris Peace Conference. *The Rising of the Tide*, only novel, published. Returns to the United States.

1920 Another collection of stories, *In Lincoln's Chair*, published. Becomes free-lance writer.

1921 *Boy Scout's Life of Lincoln*. Appointed member of President Harding's Unemployment Conference.

1922 *He Knew Lincoln, and Other Billy Brown Stories. Peacemakers—Blessed and Otherwise*, coverage of Washington Disarmament Conference, published.

1924 *In the Footsteps of the Lincolns.*

1925 *Life of Elbert H. Gary: The Story of Steel.*

1927 *A Reporter for Lincoln: The Story of Henry E. Wing.*

1930 Elected to the Author's Club; first woman member.

1932 *Owen D. Young: A New Type of Industrial Leader* published. Career as free lance slackens off but continues.

1936 *The Nationalizing of Business, 1878–1898.*

1939 *All in the Day's Work: An Autobiography.*

1943 Named consulting editor for *Letter Magazine.*

1944 Died January 6 in Bridgeport, Connecticut, hospital, of pneumonia. Buried in Titusville.

CHAPTER *1*

The Genesis of a Muckraker

THE first Muckrakers were a by-product of early twentieth-century, mass-circulation magazines. In a time of national crisis, when the trusts spawned by post–Civil War industrialism threatened to overwhelm traditional American institutions, the Muckrakers led the propaganda attack on the trusts. They accurately intuited and effectively voiced the public's alarm over the deterioration of the quality of life accompanying the new industrialism. In addition, they wholeheartedly shared the resultant moral outrage of their millions of readers; and they directed it through their writing toward government regulation of big business. Thus aroused, public opinion dictated many reforms instituted during the administration of Theodore Roosevelt. Once reforms were effected, however, the Muckrakers were themselves bluntly curbed by loss of circulation of the magazines that published them. Their readers, who had become sickened and satiated by several years of a constant flow of exposés revealing the corruption of business and politics, turned to new diversions.

Ida M. Tarbell, Lincoln Steffens, and Ray Stannard Baker inaugurated the muckraking era in 1903 with articles running concurrently in *McClure's Magazine*. Tarbell attacked industry; Steffens criticized state and municipal corruption in politics; and Baker exposed corruption in labor unions. All three pointed to industrialism as the source of corruption in American institutions. Tarbell's series, published in book form in 1904 as *The History of the Standard Oil Company,* is one of the greatest series ever to have appeared in an American magazine. Like any great work, it had a long foreground. The events and influences culminating in the book which transformed its writer from a working reporter to a national celebrity are placed into clear perspective in her autobiography, published in 1939. Tarbell did not profit from, nor exploit, her sudden fame with a hastily written book about herself; she waited until near the end of her life to summarize her experience.

I All in the Day's Work

The title of the autobiography, *All in the Day's Work*, very precisely underlines the scope and intention of a book that reflects the modesty of its author about her accomplishments, indicates that her career is the theme, and reveals her belief that work is akin to salvation. As a teen-ager in the 1870's Ida Tarbell embraced two ideas which shaped her destiny. The first was feminism: the second, the eight-hour day for the emancipation of workers, particularly of young women workers eager to escape the "bondage" of wedlock. For, while other girls prayed for a husband, Ida Tarbell "prayed to escape marriage."

To her, the "highest meaning" of work was the accomplishment of "something worth while": and in *All in the Day's Work* Tarbell surveys her career of sixty years with understated pride. Although her life was full of adventure, long and loyal friendships, and close family ties, her great source of fulfillment was her work; and the keen joy of a professional happy in her chosen field suffuses her book. Moral ballast is supplied by adherence to the traditional American values that she held eminently worthwhile—equality and independence.

All in the Day's Work clearly demonstrates that the center of Tarbell's self-identity derived from family and regional ties and that her career evolved from her critical response to them. Nothing is included in her autobiography which does not bear directly on them; for, although Tarbell moved familiarly in circles of the rich, powerful, glamorous, and talented for many years, no names are dropped nor are anecdotes introduced merely for effect. The book, written in an easy conversational style, seems rather casually organized around conventional biographical chronology; but it presents, nonetheless, a very consciously wrought portrait of its author. Never insincere, Tarbell was highly selective; but her very reticences are often revealing. Her autobiography blends sophisticated simplicity, discreet candor, strongly expressed and rather simplistic convictions, and amused yet unpatronizing awareness of the ways of the world, all faintly frosted by an aloofness which renders its author elusive.

That the ways of the world were not her ways is quite evident; but, though a careful reader senses the Puritan fist beneath the glove, her rectitude is good-humored. Her elusiveness is verified by comments of close friends and associates, who, perforce, kept whatever distance she decreed between them and her; and her very transparency shields her. A strong-minded woman, she prevailed through a tact and a compassion which were added to a charm of manner that made her incisive intelligence forgivable. What her self-portrait reveals is in full conformity with the best of Anglo-Saxon American Protestant culture. What it fails to reveal is genuine tolerance based on understanding and acceptance of life-styles other than her own. Much tolerance is there, but it is superficial, tinged with the implicit assumption of the dedicated reformer that his is the sole way of righteousness.

Slightly more than a fourth of *All in the Day's Work* is devoted to Tarbell's life before she joined the staff of *McClure's Magazine* in the summer of 1892 when she was almost thirty-five years old. She was born during the Panic of 1857 in a log "house," built by her pioneer grandfather in the Cape Cod style of his ancestors, in Erie County, Pennsylvania. Two years later the oil well drilled by Edwin L. Drake in nearby Titusville transformed the pioneering character of the region from agricultural to industrial. Then, two years after the start of the oil boom, came the Civil War, which eventually ratified the transformation.

Ida Tarbell's life was to span a complete era. She died in 1944 in her eighty-seventh year near the end of World War II, which brought with it the development of atomic energy and foreshadowed the end of the oil age into which she was born. She spent most of her long career recording the effects of industrialism on American life, but her masterpiece, *The History of the Standard Oil Company*, which went beyond merely recording history, helped significantly to make it. For this one book she will be remembered as long as there is a United States of America. The book, as the autobiography makes quite apparent, was an outgrowth of her own life and an affirmation of the values which sustained her world view.

True, Tarbell eventually abandoned the confinement of provincial Pennsylvania for Paris, where she lived in the Latin Quarter because it was "the cheapest and most practical place" in Paris for a woman with a total capital of one hundred and fifty dollars. There she studied historiography at the Sorbonne; wrote her first book, a biography of Madame Roland; and supported herself by free-lancing for American newspapers. When she joined *McClure's Magazine* in New York, her journalist's "beat" became the entire nation.

Thorough understanding of the attitudes underlying Tarbell's work consequently depends on adequate information about her formative years. Since most of her associates on *McClure's* were Midwesterners who grew up in similar circumstances, such knowledge also helps clarify the goals of the Progressive movement as interpreted by the Muckrakers, for all shared the same ethical outlook.

II *Wells, Whales, and the World's Lamps*

Herman Melville's *Moby Dick* was the swan song of the whale oil industry, for Pennsylvania oil soon replaced whales as a source for illuminating oil, the first major use of petroleum. The new industry quickly absorbed the local population; and Ida Tarbell's father, who had been prevented by the depression from emigrating to Iowa, decided to take his chances in the Titusville oil strike. A versatile frontiersman, he combined the skills of farmer, teacher, and carpenter, and the last-mentioned trade gave him his opportunity in the oil business. Producers were desperately in need of oil-storage facilities, and Tarbell quickly designed and built a wooden tank with a capacity of five hundred barrels of crude oil. His tank won immediate acceptance, and he soon had his own shop in an oil camp not then as yet dignified with the name of Rouseville.

In 1860 he built a shanty on Cherry Run Creek; and his wife and two children—Ida and a younger brother, Willie—left the placid farm life of her mother's parents to live in the shanty in the midst of the excitement of an oil boom. Ida soon discovered that an oil boom was no fun for children, since everything interesting was prohibited. Despite strict orders, she would sneak to the oil pits to try to climb the wooden derricks which loomed above the shanty like giant scarecrows. The pungent smell of oil filled the air; oil, which stained the surrounding area, killed trees, shrubs, and grass. In the wild rush for wealth, the debris from abandoned wells was left to ruin the soil and to foul the air as the new "oil farms" lined pockets and ruined land.[1]

Meanwhile, the Tarbells' prosperity enabled them to move into a new home in the green hills above Rouseville. Here the children, now including a little sister, Sarah, were encouraged to emulate the genteel, middle-class habits clung to by their parents in the face of a way of life characterized by the saloons and the brothels that catered to the tastes of the thousands of unattached men who had flocked to the region after the Civil War to seek their fortunes.[2] They included "men with and without money, with and without decency, seeking leases, jobs, . . . adventure, excitement, and swindling."[3] Since schooling in Rouseville was casual and episodic, Ida's real education came from her own reading and from her observation of the life around her, a life crude and colorful that contrasted to the Protestant sanctity of the native families, like the Tarbells, which shielded them from the alien ways of the invaders.

The reading material provided by the senior Tarbells included *Harper's Monthly* and the New York *Tribune*. In *Harper's*, Ida first encountered Charles Dickens, William Thakeray, George Eliot, and other British writers. However, she secretly supplemented such respectable writers with the contents of the *Police Gazette* which was stolen from the quarters of Mr. Tarbell's laborers. Although Ida had the best of both worlds at her disposal, her autobiography conveys the feeling that the *Police Gazette* proved more meaningful. The frank vulgarity of the women in the illustrations and the rakish virility of the men doubtless seemed truer to the life of the Oil Regions than the more subtle but less pertinent treatments of life abroad by the best British authors.

The main bulwark against the tide of corruption which threatened to inundate Rouseville was the church; and the Tarbells, born Presbyterians, joined the congregation of the First Methodist, the only church in town. The family was active in church affairs, and the extent of its activity remained vivid in Ida Tarbell's memory, as she recalled it nearly eighty years later: "We did not merely go to church, we stayed to class meeting; we went to Sunday school, where both father and mother had classes; we went to Wednesday night—or was it Thursday night?—prayer meeting. And when there was a revival we went every night."[4] Once when she was about ten she "went forward" during a revival at the preacher's urging to be saved. In the eyes of the congregation she probably was, but Tarbell recalled distinct doubt of salvation on her

part, for she had to admit that she had sought it mainly to
be on the safe side. Such motivation, she decided, could hardly
lead to heaven.[5] The honesty of her decision places her among
the world's elect, surely, if not the Lord's.

III   To Titusville and Conformity

In 1870, Ida turned a gawky thirteen. Evidently her parents
felt she had run wild long enough, for they moved to the
comparative civilization of Titusville, a town which predated
the oil boom, where Ida entered the eighth grade in the public
school. She reacted to the discipline and the regimentation
of a conventional school by establishing a notable record for
truancy. One day, when she came to class after an extended
absence, the teacher reprimanded her for her poor attendance.
"I cannot remember," she wrote in the autobiography, "that
I was ashamed or humiliated, only amazed, but something
in me asserted itself. I suppose that here a decent respect
for the opinions of mankind was born; at least I became on
the instant a model pupil."[6]

She remained a model student through high school. Most
schoolwork bored her, but she liked biology because she had
long been an amateur botanist. Like many teen-agers, she had
a religious crisis; but hers was induced by reading about Herbert Spencer's theory of evolution in *Popular Science Monthly.*
Her experience with attempted salvation at the age of ten
had indicated a certain skepticism, but she had by now concluded that formal religion was merely a form which she
scrupulously observed. She had also dispensed with the idea
of immortality, but she still believed in God and always would.
It must have been a frightening experience for a teen-age girl,
whose parents were religiously orthodox, and whose community was strongly and provincially Protestant, to struggle with
such doubts. Ida seized upon the idea of evolution as a means
to finding the key to creation.

Encouraged by her parents, both of whom were strongly
in favor of what were then called "woman's rights," she
decided to enter Allegheny College in nearby Meadville, and
to major in biology. When she learned she would be the only
girl in the class, she was undaunted; she intended to show
what a girl could accomplish academically in competition with
male students. In addition, the disproportionate sex ratio of

her class was merely of academic interest because, a true child of the woman's rights movement, she vowed never to marry.

She had a pleasant four years at Allegheny College, and she learned a good many things besides biology. Photographs reveal a tall, slim girl of five feet, eight inches, who stands with the unreposeful repose of the adolescent, not knowing quite how to arrange her long arms, bony wrists, and big hands. The youthful, rounded oval of her face softens the strength already apparent there. The face is handsome, decidedly feminine, and well proportioned except for a slight heaviness of the firm chin. Dark hair sweeps over the low forehead, a widow's peak accentuates the otherwise horizontal hairline, and dark eyebrows accent the level, observant, rather piercing light eyes; a fighter's nose juts from the brow, and the nostrils are cut high and slightly flared. The mouth is gently curved, and its youthful fullness seems appealingly vulnerable. Altogether hers is a pleasing face, like many on campuses today.

Ida soon outgrew bashfulness around boys, and was, inevitably, very popular with her classmates. One of the lasting lessons of college was the discovery that work could be pleasurable, and the conviction that it should be. This conception she learned from observing the behavior of one of her science professors, whose glowing enthusiasm for his work was infectious. It had heretofore seemed to her that "teachers, preachers, doctors, business men, all went through their day's work... with an undercurrent of uneasiness, if they found pleasure in duty. They seemed... to feel that they were not working if they were not demonstrating the Puritan teaching that labor is a curse."[7]

Ida was inclined to take the humanities rather casually because science was her real interest. However, she was promptly exposed to stinging blasts of contempt for sloppy work from one of her professors in this area of noninterest. These criticisms affected her, as had the reprimand from her eighth-grade teacher; and she learned precision in workmanship. She credited Professor George Haskins, her stinging critic, for instilling in her the dogged persistence that she always afterwards brought to her work, and she attributed to his influence her courage to express contempt, a valuable characteristic in a Muckraker.

IV   *The Standard Oil Company Bests the Independents*

For many years petroleum gathered from oil seeps had been a standby of frontier peddlers and medicine men who sold it to the gullible as a cure-all known as snake oil, among other things. The advent of petroleum in commercial quantities, however, created a fierce struggle for control of a world market eager for illuminants and lubricants. Soon the small producers and distributors of the Oil Regions were challenged and overcome by a new form of business organization which rapidly dominated and then consolidated the oil industry. This organization, the Standard Oil Company of Ohio, was headed by John Davison Rockefeller, son of a frontier peddler of patent medicines, who was destined to sell more oil than his enterprising father could ever have dreamed of.

While Ida Tarbell was still in high school, Standard Oil and a group of allied refiners from outside the Oil Regions contrived with the railroads a scheme to wrest control of the oil industry from its developers by rigging freight rates in their own favor, thus ruining their competitors, who would be financially unable to market their own oil because of prohibitive transportation rates. When the so-called South Improvement Company scheme was uncovered in 1872, the entire region erupted in violent protest; and the scheme was hastily abandoned. Caught in a tactical blunder (the discovery of the plan was accidental), the perpetrators of the plan acknowledged their error and swore to be fair thereafter. Transportation rebates, however, remained a basis for the oil monopoly that was rapidly achieved by the Standard Oil Company. The other basis was the combination of managerial efficiency and imaginative innovations in business methods originated by the corporation's numerous partners, notably by Rockefeller himself. These originators of big business seemed a strange breed in an age when businesses were predominantly small, local enterprises run by two partners or by families.

Ida's father was one of the independent producers who remained adamant against Standard Oil despite the financial reverses caused by his stand and the blighting of his future in oil. Resentment amounting to hatred of the Standard Oil methods was soon a settled state of mind in the region; and Ida Tarbell, then fifteen, was old enough to share the outraged fury of her elders over the invasion by outsiders of the industry they considered rightfully theirs. In her elders' view, right of way had been granted to the railroads by all the people; therefore, discriminatory freight rates, granted to a few, constituted a violation of the rights of the many and threatened the egalitarian tradition of American democracy.

Thus young Ida conceived, at an impressionable age, a "hatred of privilege" which never left her, and set her sights on a Goliath, the Standard Oil Company, at whom she would one day aim a Davidian slingshot. (That Standard Oil was not Goliath but Phoenix she could not have foretold.) She never accepted as valid the proposition that rebates were justified because "everybody did it." She felt as strongly in 1939 as she had in 1872 when she wrote:

Everybody did not do it. In the nature of the offense everybody could not do it. The strong wrested from railroads the privilege of preying upon the weak, and the railroads never dared give the privilege save under the promise of secrecy. In walking through the world there is a choice for a man to make. He can choose the fair and open path, the path which sound ethics, sound democracy, and the common law prescribe, or choose the secret way by which he can get the better of his fellow man.[8]

This clear-cut disjunctive proposition stated to her satisfaction the logic of the situation that she articulated some thirty years later on behalf of the people of her native region in her *History of the Standard Oil Company.*

V *A Career Begins*

Her family's reduced circumstances, as well as the unconventionality of graduate-school training for women, made it inevitable that Tarbell's first venture into the professions would be as a teacher; for that profession was the only one which welcomed women. She abandoned her dream of becoming a biologist and accepted a teaching position a short distance from Titusville at the Poland Union Seminary in Poland, Ohio. When she began her teaching duties in the fall of 1880, her class load included "two classes in each of four languages—Greek, Latin, French, and German, as well as classes in geology, botany, geometry, trigonometry."[9] In addition, she conducted refresher courses in grammar and arithmetic for elementary schoolteachers. As she soon recognized, her annual salary of five hundred dollars, with no fringe benefits and a crushing work load, amounted to a classic case of exploitation. When she quit after two years, she faced the unappealing prospect of becoming the resident spinster in her parents' home. Her luck changed unexpectedly; and she began her long career, still essentially that of a teacher, as a journalist.

For many years the Tarbell family had spent part of each summer at the Methodist camp grounds which were a short distance across the Pennsylvania state line and which were located on the shore of Lake Chautauqua, New York. During those years the Chautauqua, sponsored by the Methodist Church, had grown into a formidable cultural institution; and it offered a very popular curriculum, equivalent to four years of college courses, by correspondence. The enterprise, the Chautauqua Literary and Scientific Circle, established in 1880 a monthly magazine, *The Chautauquan,* to provide contact between students and course leaders. *The Chautauquan,* which printed portions of required course readings, annotated obscure or difficult passages in order to avoid the tons of mail previously received from puzzled readers requesting explication. When Tarbell, fresh from college and from teaching a wide variety of subjects in preparatory school, was offered a temporary job as an annotator by *The Chautauquan* editor, the Reverend Theodore L. Flood, a retired Methodist minister, she eagerly accepted and moved back to Meadville to be near the Allegheny College library and the printing press which published the magazine. Although she had been hired on an experimental basis, for the idea of annotating the publication was new, she became a permanent member of the staff. Before long she was put in charge of preparing the monthly issues of the magazine. From the foreman of the printing office she learned the skills of magazine production from copy writing to advertising—a basic training for her later tasks as an editor of *McClure's* and then of *The American Magazine.*

Editing and annotating were not enough to satisfy Tarbell: she desired to write some of the articles about current events which added interest to *The Chautauquan.* She began by writing unsigned items for a feature called "The Editor's Notebook." The drive and aggressiveness which brought her to the top of her profession were already operating, for she was soon contributing signed articles. The first of these, "The

Arts and Industries of Cincinnati," appeared in the December, 1886, issue of *The Chautauquan;* and the article reveals at least as much about the author and her readers as it does about the city.

Cincinnati is seen as if from a Puritan churchyard, and the author dutifully recounts the cultural features of the city and describes its leading industries. But the instinct for a good story, and Tarbell's unassailable rectitude—a combination that characterizes her work—prompted her to focus on the exotic foreign sins of the city. She noted with approval that Cincinnati did indeed possess a rich cultural life served by museums, parks, and band concerts; however, "morally, Cincinnati has much to learn. Its foreign population has made it a beer drinker and Sabbath breaker. The numbers of beer gardens and saloons scattered about the streets is appalling. Work in the factories and shops stops on Sunday, but to all appearances it is only to give time to frolic. The theaters, gardens, and museums are open all day. The result, however, is not so serious as might be anticipated. There are multitudes of pleasure-seekers abroad, but few carousers."[10] The author noted an effort toward improvement on the part of Sabbath keepers: "This thorough, constant, and advanced effort to Christianize the city, combined with the healthful and elevated tastes of the mass of the people, is sure to raise speedily the moral standard of Cincinnati."[11]

These excerpts from her first article contain characteristics which remained a part of Tarbell's style. Never did she split an infinitive; the insensitive ear which condoned the phrase "shops stops" persisted; the verbal imprecision which allowed beer gardens and saloons to be "scattered about the streets" as though hit by a tornado continued to appear; and "appalling" was always to indicate extreme aversion. Nevertheless, she became a fluent, lucid writer who could condense unbelievable amounts of technical information—such dry material as oil legislation or tariff regulations, for example—into a few clear, interesting pages. But her prose remained unenlivened by the felicity and flair of a more brilliant writer like her colleague on *McClure's* Lincoln Steffens. Moral indignation over injustice affecting her personally seemed capable of giving her too-bland style a touch of tartar. But, by and large, she attained the goals she established for herself: sound structure, coherence, and "beautiful clarity of expression," a quality she admired in French prose. These characteristics compensate for the similarity of organization, style, and tone found in much of her work.

An early response in *The Chautauquan* to militant feminism is in keeping with her later stand; she was disappointingly conservative to more advanced advocates of women's suffrage just before World War I. In "Women as Inventors" (March, 1887), she countered with documented evidence the rhetoric of abuse employed by the militants to hammer home their point that women lacked creativity because they were a slave class. She secured from the United States Patent Office figures to show that the number of patents issued to women since 1802, the year the office opened, was one thousand nine hundred and thirty-five. Although most of these had been for household appliances and related mechanical procedures, the Patent Office specified that true originality characterized by operation according to new principles was necessary to secure a patent. In addition, the regulations specified that the inventor must prove that "a flash of inventive genius" had inspired the invention. Tarbell's argument was that the nearly two thousand women who were certified inventive geniuses represented the hundreds of thousands of women who approached creatively their daily tasks. Tarbell's respect for facts and her scorn of theory unsubstantiated by them were undoubtedly a result of her scientific bent.

Helpful as her article may have been for the morale of readers, mainly females, it probably failed to convince the activists for women's rights, who would doubtless have loftily conceded that creativity in the kitchen existed. But the assumptions underlying Tarbell's definition of creativity differed fundamentally from those of the militant feminists, whose central issue was an equality symbolized by proven performance in the liberal arts and sciences, a male province. Production of new household gadgets was to them only additional evidence of slave mentality. To Tarbell, on the other hand, creativity itself was central and its application secondary. She remained convinced that women's place was preferably at home and that their primary sphere should be confined to the home and community—though the community eventually became the whole nation. The deep difference between Tarbell and the feminists was that, while they insisted on literal equality between the sexes, she preferred complementary equality, which cannot be quantified, but must be intuited. This interpretation of equality of the sexes came from her observation as a child of the cooperative and successful effort of the parents of the raw oil town of Rouseville to build a stable community. Consequently, the spirit of the community was for her the centrally important thing; and this spirit adapted from the agrarian past she endeavored to inculcate in all her later writings.

By 1890, Tarbell had exhausted the possibilities of *The Chautauquan* and had absorbed all its editor had to teach; moreover, the security of her position as managing editor bored her. She remembered the words of a Scotch Presbyterian minister to his congregation, the best citizens of Meadville. "You're dyin' of respectability," he had shouted, shaking his fist at them. She suddenly realized that a job could be as much a trap as marriage. She needed a new challenge, and she soon found one which occupied her fully for the next several years. The problem of the role of women in modern society interested and puzzled her. In trying to cast light on it for herself and her readers she had studied the careers of several Frenchwomen prominent in the French Revolution. She realized that her *Chautauquan* articles on women like Madame de Staël and Madame Roland were hopelessly superficial because of her insufficient knowledge and lack of source material for adequate studies.

She had come to admire French writing and the lucid rationality which produced it; and, in addition, she had great respect for French historical research techniques. At the age of thirty-two she decided to leave her native area for its opposite Paris. So attractive was her plan that three of her women friends decided to accompany her. Flood, the editor of *The Chautauquan*, gasped when she announced her intention to earn her living in France by free-lancing; he had employed her as an annotator and apparently still did not consider her a writer, despite the publication of her articles in the magazine. "You're not a writer. You'll starve," he exclaimed.[12] She knew she was not an artist, but she had determined to become a journalist. She had confidence in her intelligence and analytical ability; she could learn the rest.

After Tarbell's account of her years in Paris, *All in the Day's Work* becomes the comparatively impersonal record of the events in which she participated and the roles she played as journalist, lecturer, and personage. The nearest she came to a farm after she saw Paris was as an exurbanite in rural Connecticut, where she bought a summer place. Yet in all her public roles she remained unmistakably rooted to her past; therefore, the breath of life warms her autobiography. A nostalgic reminiscence of the area around Poland, Ohio, illustrates the interpenetration of the public and private lives of this writer as Tarbell evaluates from the vantage point of age an experience of her youth:

Years later I realized that in those two years in Poland I had had under my eyes a vivid picture of what happens to the farmer, his home, his town, his children when industry invades his land.

This Mahoning country had been so rich, so apparently stable. The men and women so loved what their forebears had done that they yielded slowly to the coal miner and the mill man, but they were giving way in the eighties. The furnace was in the backyard of the fine old houses with their ample barns; and the shaft of the coal mine, in the richest meadows. The effort to reconcile the two was [in the] making, but industry was conquering; the destruction of beauty, the breaking down of standards of conduct, the growth of love of money for money's sake, the grist of social problems facing the countryside from the inflow of foreigners and the instability of work—all this was written for him who could read. I could not read then, but I gathered . . . impressions which I realize now helped shape my future interests and thinking.[13]

Tarbell was a generation older than Sherwood Anderson. She did not perceive, as did he in *Winesburg, Ohio*, the rot beneath the surface of the old agrarian America. For her, the shimmering glow of the past was golden.

Late in her life Tarbell thus was enabled to render coherent her steadfast vision of American life, a vision less spectacular than those of contemporaries like Edward Bellamy who called upon the future to redeem the present; for she sought redemption in the American past. So pervasive was her vision that she became in the 1920's a living reminder of the best of that past to Americans seeking such a reminder in the aftermath of World War I. The task before her was to fit into her version of the American Dream the myth of Abraham Lincoln as

archetypal frontiersman, the role of women in an industrialized
democracy, and the necessity of curbing big business in order
to preserve that democracy.

CHAPTER 2

The Uses of Biography:
Popular History

IDA Tarbell once confided to a group of Cornell University women that "nearly all women who escape marriage and the schoolroom try for journalism."[1] Her own try for journalism as managing editor and part-time writer for *The Chautauquan* had revealed, however, that the pitfall of static security and comfortable conformity she had evaded in the form of marriage and teaching could also entrap the unwary journalist. Her decision to quit *The Chautauquan* and move to Paris was, therefore, a conscious choice designed to extricate her from deadening routine. Her move was a logical one, but it required maintaining the self-confidence, despite inner doubts, to confront skeptics and scoffers at home and unknown obstacles abroad.

Her plan was to pursue a course of graduate studies in history at the University of Paris; to conduct research in Parisian libraries on the French Revolutionary period, centering on the career of Madame Roland; and to support the enterprise by writing human-interest sketches of Parisian life for American newspapers. Her main project, designed as a culmination of her scholarly work, was to be a study of Madame Roland.

In a *Chautauquan* article, "Women in Journalism," she had clearly foreshadowed her subsequent career, now in its final preparatory phase. In the article she had explained the qualities necessary for a journalist: capacity for work, dependability, versatility, adaptability, no temperament, no expectations of glamor. She had concluded with an observation by Thomas Wentworth Higginson, a journalist and editor of much experience, which may well have provided the inspiration to establish her present course. Higginson had remarked about the lack of women writers of nonfiction articles for quality magazines like *The Atlantic Monthly* or *Century Magazine*.

Granting women writers' leadership in the field of best-selling fiction, he challenged them to attempt nonfiction, arguing that "the demand for general literary work of a solid and thoughtful nature demanding both scholarship and a trained power of expression—this is never very well supplied among men, and is, with few exceptions, unsupplied among American women."[2]

I Madame Roland: A Biographical Study

Tarbell's biography of Madame Roland resembles a doctoral dissertation in that it is so closely tied to a thesis which its writer is intent on constructing that the reader's attention is divided between following the flow of events and detecting flaws in a thesis which is antirevolutionary and antifeminist in the accepted meaning of feminism. The book is interesting, informative, and provocative. The scholarship is evident without being onerous; there is a selected bibliography and an index but, unfortunately, no footnotes. Though this lack is a minor omission, a modern reader used to footnoted references is sometimes left adrift, lacking a date or a source to orient him. Tarbell was most fortunate to have access to the papers of Madame Roland, which had been deposited in 1888 by her descendants in the Bibliothèque Nationale in Paris, and which had but recently been catalogued. She was, in fact, the first researcher to use them.

A journalist meets an enormous variety of people, and among the acquaintances Tarbell collected in the course of her search for feature-article stories was James Darmesteter, an eminent French scholar. He in turn introduced her to Leon Marillier, a great-great-grandson of Madame Roland and a professor in the Ecole des Hautes Etudes. Not only did he possess letters and documents which he placed at her disposal, but he also gathered her into the family circle and introduced her to his mother, who was a repository of lore about the Rolands and who could bring them to life for the American writer who had so unexpectedly arrived in their midst.

Thus, with a wealth of documentary sources and with the cooperation of the Marilliers, Tarbell was able to inject a realism into her work which differentiated it from previous romanticized biographies of her subject—biographies based largely on memoirs written in prison before Madame Roland's execu-

tion in 1793. Tarbell's intent was not to celebrate so much
as evaluate Madame Roland's experiences. Among her numerous accomplishments, the brilliant French Revolutionary
heroine had been an exemplary wife, mother, and household
manager; and Tarbell emphasizes this aspect of Madame
Roland's life. To Ida Tarbell, her subject had "passed her
happiest and most natural years" in the serene atmosphere
of her home.[3]

II A Woman of the Enlightenment

Madame Roland was born Marie-Jeanne (Manon) Phlipon
in Paris, in 1754—the same year Jean Jacques Rousseau's essay
on the origin of man's social inequality appeared. The coincidence is significant, for she was of a generation reared on
Rousseau. Her father was a prosperous engraver and jewelry
merchant, a calling which indelibly classified the Phlipons
as members of the petty bourgeoisie of small shopkeepers.
Manon spent her first two years away from her home in charge
of a nurse, a common custom of the times. Since Manon was
the only child of seven to survive, her parents may have had
additional reason for seeing that she was carefully isolated
before being restored to them. A bright, active child, she somehow had learned to read by the time she was four years old;
and her natural precociousness may have been accentuated
by her position as an only child who lacked playmates. She
read every book she could find in the house, and *Plutarch's
Lives* was one of her early favorites. In time, she had read
the books considered requisite for a Classical education; she
had, in addition, read Rousseau and the authors of the
Enlightenment, and had truly become a child of the era.

Manon delayed marriage until the age of twenty-five, having
rejected several suitors of her own class presented by her
family; then, after a long and precarious courtship, she married
Jean Marie Roland de la Platière, a member of an old and
established upper-middle-class family who was twenty years
her senior. The disparity in social class between Roland and
his future wife was a prime cause for the protracted courtship,
for that and Manon's insubstantial dowry made the match seem
a misalliance, and Roland was cautious. Finally, however, on
February 4, 1780, the marriage took place; and Manon was
elevated from her lower-class status in the only way possible.

The marriage rites were Catholic; though neither Manon nor her husband was a believer, each respected convention. A year later their only child, Marie-Thérèse-Eudora, was born.

The Rolands lived quietly and uneventfully until 1789, as if in preparation for the next four years, which found them assuming eminent positions in the Revolutionary government on the side of the moderate, bourgeois, republican Gironde faction, which was finally replaced by the radical *sans culottes* Mountain faction led by Robespierre and Danton. Madame Roland was imprisoned and executed in November, 1793, at the height of the terror. Her husband, who had escaped arrest, committed suicide when he heard the news.

Two characteristics of Tarbell as a writer are an extraordinary sense of place and a strong preference for dramatizing situations by focusing on individuals, and both are apparent in *Madame Roland.* In the opening chapters—concerned with Madame Roland's early life; eighteenth-century Paris, particularly the Point Neuf quarter where Manon spent her childhood: and Le Clos, where she spent the most carefree times of her married life—vividly evoked portrayals are found. Madame Roland is, of course, the central character of the account of the revolution until 1793, which comprises the major portion of the biography. The focus is on her part in welding the Girondist faction; in carrying it beyond the endorsement of the constitutional monarchy into advocacy of a republic; and in stiffening the opposition of the remainder of the Gironde, after the execution of the king, to any compromise with the extremist Mountain party led by Robespierre and Danton, toward whom Madame Roland felt an ineradicable repugnance.

Tarbell's conclusion was that the Girondists were amateurs in politics and that their idealism set them against the pragmatic compromise symbolized by the constitutional monarchy, which could have worked with their support. Their idealism carried them instead into a republicanism which was easily taken out of their genteel bourgeois control by radical extremists who were professional agitators, and who also possessed a decisive power base among the lower classes that were disliked and distrusted by the Gironde and that promptly liquidated the Gironde in the ensuing Terror. Whether the juggernaut set in motion in 1789 could have been stopped at the stage of constitutional monarchy is debatable, but Tarbell's contention is interesting because it reveals her own pragmatism and her willingness to settle for half a loaf in the interests of orderly evolution. Necessarily, it reveals also her aversion to revolution; it seemed to her irrational and nihilistic—to be a fever which ravages the body politic, runs its course, and leaves things basically unchanged.

By temperament, then, Tarbell was unsympathetic to the idealism and romantic enthusiasm of Madame Roland. Her biography idealizes Madame Roland in her domestic role, but fails to take into account the restless brilliance, ambition, and love of power which possessed Manon from her childhood and which led to personal accomplishments resulting in an advantageous marriage that provided a platform for her swift leap into fame when the opportunity of the Revolution presented itself, a feat impossible for a woman—particularly an eighteenth-century one—unless she gained power through manipulating influential men. But Madame Roland's popular title, "Queen of the Gironde," also indicated her skill in manipulating the men of the upper-middle-class intelligentsia who comprised her husband's circle—a skill enhanced by her utter sincerity concerning the revolutionary cause that provided the context of the manipulation.

The many quotations from Madame Roland's correspondence and memoirs in the biography present her as a woman of unusual brilliance, charm, and force, whose thirst for eminence happened to coincide with a cause in which she believed, and which she rode to the crest. Her love of power is clearly demonstrated, but her integrity is equally obvious. Rather than compromise at the end with the brutally violent extremists (whom, in any case, it is doubtful she could have manipulated), she chose to back François Buzot in a last desperate attempt to avert the triumph of her radical opponents. The attempt failed, and in the end Manon transcended failure in the only way left—by enduring imprisonment and execution with a degree of grace and nobility that demonstrated beyond question the strength of character and conviction which sustained her.

This is one reader's interpretation of Madame Roland based upon the Tarbell biography. Tarbell's own interpretation, however, is somewhat different; and it is biased by her preference for Madame Roland's domestic role and by her disapproval of Manon's public one. Tarbell concluded that Madame Roland's political activities had been motivated solely by emotional attachment, first to her husband, then to Buzot. And indeed, love for both men is vehemently expressed in letters, though that for Buzot was epistolary only. But it seems unlikely that either love was untainted by an admixture of personal ambition.

The point is that Tarbell oversimplified her treatment of Madame Roland when she concluded that Madame Roland's political actions were motivated solely by love; moreover, Tarbell then generalized from that one assumed instance that the same thing holds true for all women—that their only interest in politics is that of serving their men. Tarbell speculated with little basis in cold fact that, had Madame Roland been willing to temporize with Danton after the rise of the Paris Commune in the summer of 1793, the Gironde could have maintained a moderating influence on the course of the revolution. But, according to Tarbell, she would not temporize because: "A woman in love is never a good politician. The sentiment she experiences lifts her above all ordinary considerations. All relations seem petty beside the supreme union which she desires. The object of her passion becomes the standard of her feelings towards others.... Even if she be a cool-headed woman with a large sense of humor and see that her championship [of her lover] is illogical, she cannot give it up."[4] Since Tarbell, throughout the biography, documented the fact that Madame Roland exerted a compelling influence on her husband, Buzot, Bosc, and other Girondist intimates, her reasoning will not stand up under close scrutiny.[5]

The other serious flaw in the book is that Tarbell applies the standards of her own time and place to the past and to a different *milieu* from her nineteenth-century, provincial American one. One example suffices: Tarbell remarks that Madame Roland's memoirs were consciously modelled on Rousseau's *Confessions* with the result that "she related some experiences which good sense and taste, not to say delicacy, ought to have forbidden her to repeat to any one, above all, to the public.... When she came to writing her life, she dragged to light unimportant and unpleasant details because

Rousseau had had the bad taste to do the same before her. The naïveté, with which these things are told, will convince any one that cares to examine the Memoirs that they mean nothing but she had taken the foolish engagement to tell everything she could remember about her life."[6]

If one examines the *Mémoires*, however, it develops that Madame Roland attached crucial importance to an incident in her childhood which Tarbell passes over without comment. When Madame Roland was about ten years old, a teen-age apprentice of her father who lived with the family crudely attempted to seduce her. As a result of this introduction of the lonely, suggestible, bookish young girl to sex, she reacted by becoming extremely religious throughout the early years of her adolescence; in addition the event caused, according to Madame Roland, her great timidity toward men and resulted in her late marriage at the age of twenty-five.[7] To a present-day reader, Madame Roland's account of her youthful experience seems highly relevant to the course of her life. She is explicit about the incident and its aftereffects without being in the least indelicate. She realizes, in a way Tarbell perhaps would not admit, the interrelationship of her emotional and mental development.

The conventions of the nineteenth century led Tarbell to ignore the trauma which apparently precipitated in her young subject what amounted to a religious hysteria so marked that her parents sent her to a convent boarding school for a year. Tarbell merely reports of the experience that the "profane atmosphere" of the Phlipon home disturbed Manon's religious devotions and that, at their daughter's request, the parents sent the child away to a convent. Tarbell's account of the incident is, by and large, accurate; but it reveals limitations in her as a writer which too often led to superficiality in treating the psychological dimensions of the subjects of her biographies. The conventions of the twentieth century prompt applause for Madame Roland's insight in reporting her premature and disturbing sexual encounter, but those of nineteenth-century Protestant America forbade Tarbell's even mentioning it.

Madame Roland was completed in the summer of 1894, but it was not published until after the success of Tarbell's biography of Napoleon, which ran in *McClure's* from November,

1894, through June, 1895, persuaded William C. Brownell of Scribners that it would sell.[8] Unfortunately, it did not; but it is superior in depth and complexity to the popular biography of Napoleon which made Tarbell famous.

III *A New Breed of Journalists*

S. S. McClure, who was soon to dazzle the magazine world with his revolutionary development of mass-circulation methods, hired Ida Tarbell for his staff after he had noticed one of her articles, sent to McClure's Syndicate for newspaper distribution, and had selected her to be an occasional contributor for *McClure's Magazine.* While she was quietly completing work on her biography of Madame Roland and was once again in Titusville, Ida Tarbell received an urgent summons in August, 1894, from McClure, who needed a biographer for a series in *McClure's* on the life of Napoleon, since the first installment had already been announced for November. McClure was convinced, on the strength of a few articles and an as yet unpublished biography, that the unknown thirty-seven-year-old spinster he had hired on a hunch could write the series; but the idea seemed laughable to her. She had spent three years on *Madame Roland,* and she was now commanded to start producing, in less than two months, a biography of Napoleon Bonaparte!

But McClure, driven by desperation because of a breakdown in negotiations with the writer originally chosen for the job, insisted. Impetus for the series had been the opportunity not only to profit from the then current interest in Napoleon but also to publish in the biography portraits owned by Gardiner Green Hubbard, a rich Napoleon *aficionado* who lived in Washington, D.C. McClure had commissioned Robert Sherard, great-grandson of William Wordsworth, to write a biography. Unsurprisingly, in view of his ancestry, Sherard's biography of Napoleon was highly uncomplimentary; and Hubbard refused to let it appear with his pictures. McClure secured Tarbell for the assignment with the promise of a forty-dollar-a-week salary, the cooperation of Hubbard, and freedom in the use of materials held by the Congressional Library. Half-amused, she accepted; and by October she had completed the first chapter.[9]

Hubbard liked it, though she herself regretted its sketch-

iness. Her years of study of the Revolution in Paris had embold-
ened her to seize this unexpected chance; and, with her usual
decisiveness, she plunged ahead, despite her inner hesitation
in the face of what she considered hasty scholarship. Her decision is conclusive evidence that the inner tug of war between
student and journalist was over and that Thomas Wentworth
Higginson's challenge to women to write serious nonfiction
articles for periodicals was about to be met by a scholarly
woman journalist, the herald of a new breed of journalists
of both sexes.

Despite its seeming impetuosity, McClure's plan for the
Napoleon biography was carefully thought out. In 1840, Louis
Phillippe, Bourbon successor to the Bonapartes, had ordered
Napoleon's remains returned to French soil from Elba. Shortly
thereafter, as if pursued by the ghost of the first Napoleon,
Louis was replaced on the throne by his nephew Napoleon
III. Following that event, the Napoleon cult became literary,
and had reached its height by the 1890's in France and in
the United States. As McClure gloatingly recalled, "In
November the *Century Magazine* began its *Life of Napoleon*,
by Professor [William Milligan] Sloane, which they had been
preparing for years, and the same month we began our *Life
of Napoleon*, got up, as it were, overnight. Within a few months
our circulation rose from 40,000 to 80,000."[10]

McClure's editorial genius prompted transferring quality in
content—heretofore limited to class magazines of limited circulation—to mass magazines; for he sensed an audience for
good articles among people who would not pay the price of
the quality periodicals. In 1893, the *Century* sold for thirty-five
cents, a considerable price in those days; but the first issue
of *McClure's*, that of May, 1893, sold for fifteen cents, and
that price was lowered a year later to ten cents. The substitution
of a much cheaper photoengraving process for the expensive
wood engraving one previously used for magazine illustrations
also made the lower price possible. Though sold at the same
price as *Munsey's Magazine*, cheap alike in price and contents,
the quality of *McClure's* was comparable to that of the class
magazines but far less stodgy. During the twenty years of
McClure's editorship the magazine was as fine a publication
of its kind as any before or since. Thus *McClure's* offered
Ida Tarbell the excitement of pioneering in a new field of

journalism literally created by S. S. McClure, for which her previous experience ideally suited her.[11]

IV *Life of Napoleon Bonaparte*

The Hubbard collection was the *pièce de résistance* of *McClure's* Napoleon series, but Tarbell's text provided continuity. In contrast to Sloane's leisurely biography that was running concurrently in the *Century*, hers moved swiftly, often changing focus to feature historical highlights rather than meticulously developing the background of their emergence. The portraits and other illustrations, which contributed a vitalizing immediacy, totaled two hundred; and seventy-five of them were portraits from the Hubbard collection. They ranged from one of Napoleon as a thin, intense, surly-looking Italian youth of fifteen, to the idealized portraits of him as emperor, looking like one of the Caesars; to one following his abdication, which reveals him slumped disconsolately, a fat, dumpy little man who still has the intense, brooding expression of his youth; to the priestlike serenity and resignation of the death mask. The feature was properly advertised as a "a great Pictorial Life of Napoleon"; in addition, it conformed to McClure's editorial policy that every feature "must entertain" as well as be judged "instructive or uplifting, or it does not go into the magazine."

The biography itself was concluded in the April, 1895, issue of *McClure's;* but the first six installments were followed by two others in the May and June issues: the first described Napoleon's reburial in Paris; the second was a historical account of the Louisiana Purchase of 1803. The total text, which ran to a hundred and fifty-six pages, was printed around the profuse illustrations. The first installment of twenty-four pages rapidly reviewed the events of Napoleon's life from 1769, the year of his birth, to 1795, when he became General of the Army of the Interior under the Directory. The second installment carries the narrative to 1812, the year of the Moscow reverse. The facts are presented baldly, with little room for development; the contents are jumbled together with little coherence; but the relationship to the accompanying illustrations is indicated by subtitles like "Napoleon's Love for His Wife," "Summary of the Italian Campaign," and "Napoleon's Rules of War." The next four articles enlarge on material introduced in the first two, thereby fleshing out the narrative.

Tarbell's skill in simplifying masses of data and her swift narrative style assured the popularity of the biography. It appeared in book form, somewhat amplified and more coherently organized, immediately following its conclusion in the magazine; and the work was reprinted many times. There were six reprintings in 1905 alone, and the latest was in 1923. Like the serial, the book is organized around the Hubbard collection. The portraits are grouped into four significant periods of Napoleon's career: 1796–1797 was entitled "Napoleon the General"; 1801–1804, "Napoleon the Statesman and Lawgiver"; 1804–1812, "Napoleon the Emperor"; 1812–1815, "Decline and Fall of Napoleon." A lively, accurate, and informative overview, the book conveys with much sympathy, a sense of the tragic sweep of Napoleon's career; and strong emphasis is given to his central role in completing the work of the Revolution by modernizing France, a role Tarbell considered his most important one. She approved of this contribution, for Napoleon acted, in this instance, as an essentially constructive agent of social evolution rather than of revolution: lacking the nihilistic destructiveness she had condemned in the activities of Madame Roland's associates and in those who had seized power from the Girondists, Napoleon's domestic measures represented what might have occurred earlier if the constitutional monarchy of Louis XVI had not been sabotaged.

V *"An Empress in Name, Never in Soul"*

The second edition of the *Life of Napoleon* (1901) includes a short biography of Josephine Bonaparte. Its tone is indicated by the frontispiece, a photograph of a statue of her as empress by the sculptor Vital-Dubray. He reproduced in marble the appeal which made her the mistress of the Vicomte de Barras, whose efforts saved her from execution in 1794 during the Terror, which had been the fate of her husband, Alexandre de Beauharnais. Barras also encouraged the match with Napoleon, whom she married in 1796. Vital-Dubray's statue emphasizes Josephine's physical grace, and stresses her fragile femininity combined with a restrained voluptuousness, which doubtless aided her at thirty-two to cause the twenty-six-year-old Napoleon to fall violently in love with her.

Tarbell's Josephine is pleasure-loving, amoral, charmingly

amiable, indolent, and, in contrast to Madame Roland, none too bright. Like Madame Roland, who in Tarbell's view had been miscast as Queen of the Gironde, Josephine was unsuited to become empress of France, since nature had designed her to be queen of a simple household. Tarbell—disregarding Josephine's failure to provide an heir for the throne, or other reasons of state for Napoleon's divorcing her—insisted that, had Josephine remained "true, no other woman could have existed for him. Such is the strange exclusiveness of a nature brutal, sweet, and strong like Napoleon's."[12] Josephine's unfaithfulness to her husband was repugnant to Tarbell's rigid middle-class morality; to her and to her readers, Caesar's wife was the only suitable model for empresses—and for the rest of humanity as well.

Both Napoleon and Josephine were, in Tarbell's view, products of an environment which accepted as the highest goals the achievement of power and the special privilege which automatically accompanies it. Such goals were antithetical to Tarbell's internalized egalitarianism. In her interpretation, a corrupt social order had engendered such goals, had perverted Napoleon's capacity for leadership, and had also led to Josephine's misuse of her major endowment, her sex. Because of Josephine's exemplary conduct following her divorce, Tarbell conceded that, despite Josephine's "shallow" pleasure seeking, "it would be unjust to judge her by the orderly standards of present-day Anglo-Saxon morality" since she had "finally attained rectitude of conduct" after the trials of being "an Empress in name, never in soul."[13]

For all Tarbell's concessions to her own and her public's sentimentality and to "Anglo-Saxon morality," she achieved her goal as biographer in the portrayals of both the emperor and the empress. Sloane, the *Century's* Napoleon biographer, complimented her on her work, in terms that exceeded mere politeness: "I am not so sure that all the time you want to take, all the opportunity to indulge your curiosity and run here and there on bypaths, to amuse yourself, to speculate and doubt, contribute to the soundness or value of a biography. I have often wished that I had had, as you did, the prod of necessity behind me, the obligation to get it out at a fixed time, ... no time to idle, to weigh, only to set down. You got something that way—a living sketch."[14] Professor Sloane's

comment accurately pinpointed Tarbell's intention of bringing
an era vividly to life by focusing on a shaper of it. In addition,
the illustrations were treated as a functional component of
the whole—a treatment which fulfilled the terms of her
assignment.

Her central purpose, in the Napoleon biography as in
Madame Roland, was more historical than biographical.
Through Madame Roland and through Napoleon she described
and evaluated the early and the concluding phases of the
French Revolution, respectively. In *Madame Roland,* she had
investigated for her own enlightenment the worth of revolution
and the value of women's contributions to public life, and
she denied each. In the *Life of Napoleon,* she exploited the
public's curiosity about Napoleon to teach history and, whether
consciously or not, to reinforce American complacency regarding European moral and political decadence. Her history of
the French Revolution was related with an unmistakably
American accent.

Tarbell's summation of Napoleon's characteristics is based
on psychological realism. In her view, Napoleon was no super-
man; but he possessed extraordinary intelligence and was an
excellent administrator who personally supervised the carrying
out of plans which were audacious beyond the grasp of more
ordinary men. Meticulous about details, he did not leave too
many to subordinates; but he could delegate authority wisely.
He was blessed with a remarkable physical resiliency which
enabled him to work long hours on little sleep. A last characteristic, however, she considered a fatal flaw: the presumption
that he was a law unto himself.[15] She concluded that Napoleon
was "the greatest genius of his time, perhaps of all time; yet
he lacked the crown of greatness—that high wisdom born of
reflection and introspection which knows its own powers and
limitations, and never abuses them; that fine sense of proportion which holds the rights of others in the same solemn reverence it demands for its own."[16] In her next assignment for
McClure's, a biography of Abraham Lincoln, she fashioned
for him the "crown of greatness" she had withheld from
Napoleon.

CHAPTER 3

The Uses of Biography:
Didactic Myth

PARALLELING the Napoleon boom in the late nineteenth century was another created by unflagging interest in Abraham Lincoln. The interest in Lincoln had been stimulated by publication in the *Century Magazine* of an abridged version of *Abraham Lincoln: A History* by John G. Nicolay and John Hay. After completion of the serial in 1890, the *Century* then published the Nicolay and Hay biography in ten volumes, establishing them as the official guardians of the Lincoln tradition; for they were the sole authors who had been given access to his father's papers by Robert Todd Lincoln. In return, he had exacted control over their manuscript and had heavily censored their account of Lincoln's frontier youth.[1] In addition, he had stipulated that the Lincoln papers would not be available again until twenty-six years after his death. The Nicolay and Hay biography was supplemented by their edition in 1894 of the twelve-volume *Collected Works*.

But the Lincoln legend could not be contained behind even these formidable ramparts. The alert S. S. McClure envisioned a wider market. If the Nicolay and Hay series had increased the *Century's* circulation, he reasoned, what might a similar feature do for *McClure's*? If Napoleon had staved off failure for the magazine, Lincoln could ensure its success. However, the idea encountered resistance from his staff, which thought that the current supply of Lincoln articles and Civil War features in other publications was glutting the market, and which was slower than McClure in recognizing the analogy between the success of the recent Napoleon series and the possibility of benefits for *McClure's* from a Lincoln series. To McClure, who was convinced that his readers would also benefit from reminders of the American virtues Lincoln embodied, combination of market and mission was irresistible; and a Lincoln series was announced. Circulation rose immediately to reach three hundred thousand after the series began, thereby increasing the revenue from advertising to the highest figure thus far recorded in magazine history.[2]

I *The best laid plans* . . .

The original plan for the Lincoln series was to publish documents, photographs, other illustrations, and signed reminiscences of Lincoln's contemporaries, which were to be edited by Ida Tarbell. She followed Lincoln's trail from Kentucky through Indiana to Illinois, absorbed the atmosphere of places where he had lived and worked, took photographs, interviewed those who remembered him, and searched in newspaper files, courthouses, and attics for fresh documents. Meanwhile, *McClure's* requested readers for materials, which promptly arrived in enormous quantities. Tarbell and J. McCan Davis of Springfield, Illinois, then began the long process of verifying all leads.

It soon became apparent that the mass of Lincoln material was too fragmentary to be reduced to coherence by mere editing. Tarbell was then assigned to write a biography of Lincoln up to 1858, one which would incorporate as much as possible the fragments so painstakingly collected and verified.[3] When she approached John Nicolay for unused material, he brusquely refused to provide any; indeed, he was openly resentful. "You are invading my field," he complained bitterly. "You write a popular *Life of Lincoln* and you do just so much to decrease the value of my property."[4] As he viewed it, allowing a "girl" to write a Lincoln biography was absurd enough, but the effort to encompass Lincoln or his times by a writer who was too young to have known either presented an insuperable obstacle.[5]

That biographies by Lincoln's contemporaries were, on the contrary, beginning to present such obstacles seemed more likely; and fresh interpretations by the generation following Lincoln were being called for. The Tarbell interpretation was foreshadowed in "Lincoln's Place in History," an article by John Coleman Adams, a Universalist minister born in Massachusetts, in the February, 1894, issue of the *Century*. It seemed safe to Adams to predict that Lincoln's place was secure as the greatest President since Washington. And, he added, "it is by no means heresy to see in Lincoln and in Ralph Waldo Emerson types of American greatness more thoroughly our own than even that of Washington." Moreover, the time had come, thought Adams, to measure "our man of the West in his world relations"; for, in his opinion, the Civil War had corrected a counterevolutionary drift on the part of the South that had threatened to undo twenty-five centuries of slow but steady progress toward peace and democracy which had culminated in "the American Union" as the "highest political embodiment of Christianity."[6]

The need for a new, concise biography had previously been noted by Lincoln's contemporary, Carl Schurz, in a widely read review of the Nicolay and Hay biography in the June, 1891, *Atlantic Monthly* which had been reprinted by Houghton, Mifflin & Company. Schurz complained that the ten-volume work of Nicolay and Hay was neither history nor biography; it was an unsuccessful attempt to combine both. He granted its value and importance, but he characterized it as tedious and redundant and as heavily moralistic and far too uncritically eulogistic. Previous biographers, according to Schurz, had allowed awe to overcome objectivity. "No American," he declared impatiently, "can study the character of Abraham Lincoln without being carried away by sentimental emotions. We are always inclined to idealize that which we love—a state of mind very unfavorable to the exercise of sober critical judgment."[7]

To Schurz, who had known the President well, Lincoln, "one of the greatest of Americans and the best of men," little needed falsifying idolatry. As a European, Schurz was more aware than other commentators of the apparent incongruity of Lincoln's birth in a log cabin with his achievement of political heights; but he accepted it as a condition common in American experience. Adopting the current view of Lincoln's origins, he placed his beginning as even farther from the heights than the traditional lowly cabin. "We may search in vain among our celebrities," he wrote, "for one whose origin and early life equalled Abraham Lincoln's in wretchedness."[8] His father, according to Schurz, had been typical "shiftless and improvident" frontier white trash; his mother had been coarsened, soured, and finally killed by the "toil and care" of managing her "squalid household" by the time Lincoln was nine years old.

In her biography, Tarbell sustained the Emersonian note sounded by John Coleman Adams and also his emphasis on Lincoln as the savior of democracy. She provided the conciseness longed for by Schurz, and she compensated for the overdramatic stress by previous interpreters on the misery of Lincoln's youth by bringing to bear her own youthful experience in a pioneer area, thereby putting Lincoln's in clearer perspective. She, in turn, promulgated a myth which has endured of the Anglo-American frontiersman who was born to save the "American Union."

Undeterred by her dismissal from Nicolay, Tarbell next sought help from Robert Todd Lincoln; for she hoped to gain access to the jealously guarded Lincoln papers. He graciously invited her to his home in Chicago for tea; but resisting the Tarbell charm which made her feared among Lincoln students, who often found themselves parting with valuable treasures as a result of her persuasiveness, Lincoln did not allow her to see the papers. He did give her, however, a previously unpublished daguerreotype of his father taken in 1848 when he was about thirty-nine, the earliest known portrait of him. In this case, one picture was truly worth a thousand words; for it contradicted the popular image of him as a shambling backwoodsman with unkempt hair and a slack jaw who wore a ragged shirt and greasy coonskin cap. Instead, it showed him conventionally dressed, his hair was short and neatly combed, and his expression was strikingly like that of Ralph Waldo Emerson—dreamy yet virile, poetic yet craggily noble. Such a portrait served not only as the perfect complement to that of the young Lincoln soon to emerge in the Tarbell biography, but also as frontispiece to the first Lincoln article in the November, 1895, issue of *McClure's*. It attracted much attention, for it heraled a revisionist interpretation of Lincoln's early years.[9]

II   The Life of Abraham Lincoln

All in all, Tarbell unearthed over three hundred previously uncollected documents, mostly speeches, letters, or telegrams; and all but one of them proved to be genuine. They included such items as a newspaper copy of Lincoln's first speech, facts about his life in New Salem and Springfield, and a certified copy of his marriage certificate; and all are listed in the appendix of the published biography, where they take up one hundred and ninety-four pages of the second volume. Volume I recounts Lincoln's life until his nomination for the presidency in 1860; and it ran in *McClure's* for a year, from November, 1895, through the following November. The popularity of this series prompted a second one, which took the account from 1860 to Lincoln's assassination. This series, Volume II of the published biography, appeared in *McClure's* from December, 1898, through the following September.

The Life of Abraham Lincoln is structured like a play; for its thirty-one chapters fall into three acts: the first eleven chapters end with Lincoln's marriage in 1842 and his subsequent election to Congress; the next ten carry the action up to his election to the presidency in 1860; and the final ten chapters complete the drama with his assassination. The first third is the best because Tarbell was on familiar ground in retailing Lincoln's frontier background; as a result, she was able to incorporate the wealth of anecdotes available to her to characterize her subject. Because she herself had grown up in a similar environment, she could realistically visualize Lincoln's early years without shocking the sensibilities of readers used to gentler living. Her feeling for the circumstances of his frontier experience enabled her to weave together the innumerable reminiscences she had available into a coherent narrative that made believable Lincoln's development from a Yahoo to a man of destiny.

She traced for her readers a line of development from the Puritans of Massachusetts Bay to the White House which obliterated any rough frontier edges that would have offended the sensibilities of her readers. William H. Herndon, Lincoln's law partner, had written a realistic account of Lincoln's early years; but its rough and ready realism had not appealed to the public. Tarbell's genteel realism carried the right touch for her time.

She used very skillfully the wealth of anecdotes at her disposal to characterize Lincoln and to persuade her readers that a great politician was of necessity a complex personality. Such an anecdote provides the finishing touch to her portrait of Lincoln just prior to his reentering politics in the 1850's. The episode concerns the abandonment of law as a profession by Ralph Emerson, a young lawyer of Rockford, Illinois. Emerson,

who was troubled by a conflict he was unable to resolve, asked
the more experienced Lincoln's opinion:

The young man had seen much in the practice of his chosen profession
which seemed to him unjust, and he had begun to feel that the law
was incompatible with his ideals. One evening, after a particularly
trying day in court, he walked out with Lincoln. Suddenly turning
to his companion, he said, "Mr. Lincoln, I want to ask you a question.
Is it possible for a man to practice law and always do by others
as he would be done by?" Lincoln's head dropped on his breast,
and he walked in silence for a long way; then he heaved a heavy
sigh. When he finally spoke, it was of a foreign matter. "I had my
answer," said Mr. Emerson, "and that walk changed the course of
my life."[10]

Tarbell traced Lincoln's ancestry to Hingham, Massachusetts, where Samuel Lincoln had arrived in 1637 as an
indentured servant. The ancestry of Nancy Hanks, Lincoln's
mother, also stemmed from early New England. Members of
both families began migrating westward in the seventeenth
century. Such ancestry conferred roots and respectability. Tarbell was anxious to remove the stigma of illegitimacy from
Nancy's birth to add to the respectability, and she argued per-
suasively for it. (When the evidence later was to the contrary,
she acknowledged her error.) Her point, of course, was to establish the existence of an unexceptionably conventional background for her subject by stripping away the aura of cretinism
previously associated with his origins in order to rehabilitate
not only the Lincolns but also all frontier folk, who were often
lightly dismissed as no-accounts by stay-at-homes.

Her thesis was that there was a necessary connection
between Lincoln's greatness and his background. She was in
agreement with James Fenimore Cooper's contention in *The
Prairie* that the pioneers' self-sufficient pride reflected their
ancestry as did their blind, relentless drive to settle farther
and farther to the west. Cooper, writing in the 1820's, sought
to clarify this drive and the pride that sustained it:

The Anglo-American is apt to boast, and not without reason, that
his nation may claim a descent more truly honorable than that of
any other people whose history is to be credited. Whatever might
have been the weaknesses of the original colonists, they were sincerely pious, and, consequently, honest. The descendants of these

simple and single-minded provincials have been content to reject the ordinary artificial means by which honors have been perpetuated in families, and have substituted a standard which brings the individual himself to the ordeal of public estimation, paying as little deference as may be to those who have gone before him.[11]

Tarbell shared Cooper's implicit assumption that being born an "Anglo-American" was in itself suffcient distinction for any man.

The middle third of *The Life of Abraham Lincoln* achieves dramatic tension through emphasis on the ideological conflict between Lincoln and Stephen A. Douglas over the extension of slavery, which reached a climax in the Lincoln-Douglas debates which focused national attention on Lincoln and paved the way for his nomination for the presidency in 1860. The last third of the biography, although swift moving and smoothly paced, is nevertheless a flat account of the presidential years. The narrative starts well with the contest for dominance between Lincoln and Seward, but it soon lapses into a loosely connected recital of historical events. The war years become a mere chronicle because Lincoln's motivation is never explored, as it is in the opening section, nor is there perceptible character development. Anecdotes are as numerous as before, but they fail to cohere into any totality of impression. Herbert Hoover once commented to Tarbell that he believed Volume II of her Lincoln biography lacked power because of her own lack of war experience. He was perhaps right; for, when she brought her own experience into play in the early part of the book, she was able to convey convincingly the frontier locale. New Salem, Illinois, surely could not have been ruder or more rugged than the Rouseville of her early childhood.[12]

II *Ida Tarbell's Reputation as a Lincoln Biographer*

The Nation's reviewer pinpointed the enduring contribution of Ida Tarbell's *The Life of Abraham Lincoln* when he commented that the new facts and her interpretation based upon them added a new dimension to Lincoln studies. He noted too the documentation which enabled her to satisfy "in an honest way" public curiosity about Lincoln's life.[13] Since Tarbell was the first of a new generation to write a Lincoln biography, she brought to the project a comparatively open mind. Previous writers had known him, their bias for or against him had distorted their views, but most had been unduly romantic. The "I-knew-him-when" realism of William Herndon, Lincoln's law partner, had, on the contrary, proved unpalatable to the public; and his biography had sold poorly. Tarbell had used much material from Herndon's papers after Robert Lincoln's refusal to let her use the Lincoln papers, but she had softened the effect to achieve a realism analogous to the brand that William Dean Howells practiced in his fiction, for both writers gauged their public accurately, and neither ventured beyond the bounds of what was permissable. She mentions Lincoln's flaws but does not dwell on them; she tends, instead, to lay stress on the essential greatness beneath, a greatness she never questions.

Her purpose had been to present to the public neither a prophet nor a seer of democracy but a representative man in the Emersonian sense. In her view, Lincoln had succeeded, not through a decree of destiny, but, as had Napoleon, because of innate qualities of mind and temperament. Nature had not "made him a saint. His lofty moral courage in the Civil War was the logical result of his life-long fidelity to his conscience."[14] In this manner she heeded Carl Schurz's pleas to refrain from deifying Lincoln and presented him clearly, for the first time, as a manifestation of indigenous greatness, thereby reaffirming the values of the old America at a time when they were seemingly ineffective in countering the changes sweeping over the nation. Perhaps this quality made the book so enormously popular, for her interpretation, which caught hold and endured, was given additional scope and power by Carl Sandburg in his biography of Lincoln, written in the 1930's in another time of national stress.

Tarbell's biography, which remained a popular favorite until the 1930's, is still a standard source; but recent scholarship and the release of the Lincoln papers in 1947 have largely superseded what was a pioneer work in Lincoln studies. Benjamin P. Thomas, an eminent academic Lincoln scholar, said of Tarbell that, like Lincoln, she "saw democracy as a spiritual faith, not as a matter of law or system, . . . [her] faith in democracy was no less strong than Lincoln's, and he saw it as 'the last, best hope on earth.' "[15] Thomas gracefully qualified Tarbell's scholarship by pointing out her position as an advocate of an ideology. He placed her midway between the "idealists," whose Lincoln biographies were unreliable in fact and interpretation, and the contemporary scholars, whose aim is objectivity. He classified her as an "idealistic realist" who was inclined toward the sentimental. Yet, he added, she "never put sentiment above evidence," though she was apt to be "uncritically laudatory" in her estimate of Lincoln.[16]

All in all, Thomas rates Tarbell as more a realist than an idealist, for she could not fairly be called a Lincoln "idolator." He summed up her contribution as that of a popularizer, "the pioneer scientific investigator whose work foretold the revelation of Lincoln as he really was," and whose "comprehension of Lincoln was her most precious literary legacy."[17] Thomas included her with the literary interpreters of Lincoln, rather than the scholars; and he pointed out that Lincoln had been a problematical subject for academic historians. Scholarly scrutiny, he explained, had left unaltered Lincoln's "faith in democracy, his high moral character and courage, his great common sense, his sympathy, his moderation and self-effacement, his keen feeling for popular opinion, his sane, conservative approach to the manifold aspects of slavery."[18] Yet the man himself eluded them, thought Thomas. He concluded that a literary treatment of Lincoln, such as that of Tarbell or Sandburg, was liable to romantic excess, but he also admitted that scholarly realism alone could not explain him.

But Tarbell had not been writing for historians. Her immediate purpose had been to popularize Lincoln in a biography as factually accurate as research could make it and to give currency to an interpretation of him as the average American writ large. Thus she, a journalist, more so perhaps than even the poet Walt Whitman, created a myth, or rather articulated and made a part of American consciousness a subliminal folk myth. Such an achievement as that is granted to few writers. The cultural bias which led her to bestow the "crown of greatness" on Lincoln the democrat rather than on Napoleon the dictator was a limitation which characterized her; but it was counterbalanced by a characteristic asset—the restraint that kept her from fashioning Lincoln's crown of greatness into a Christ-like crown of thorns.

IV   *A Lincoln Disciple*

The four years Tarbell had spent on *The Life of Abraham Lincoln* had aroused her desire to keep before her readers of a less heroic age the memory of Lincoln's moral grandeur; and she had the wherewithal to carry out her desire. The hundreds of Lincoln reminiscences accumulated during her four years of research provided material for magazine articles about Lincoln for many more years; and Tarbell, with the thrift of a professional, obtained full value for the labor of collecting them. A story about some homely, inspirational incident in Lincoln's life was a predictable feature, well into the 1930's, of the February issue of one of a number of popular magazines. Tarbell had a flair for anecdotes in dialect and an affectionate understanding of the Midwestern prairie folk of the same stock as her own. Her Lincoln articles were well received, and many were collected. *He Knew Lincoln* (1907) featured Lincoln at the cracker barrel with storekeeper Billy Brown as narrator; *Father Abraham* (1909) recounted tales of Lincoln among the soldiers; another collection of Billy Brown stories followed in 1924; *In Lincoln's Chair* (1920) contained anecdotes concerning his religious views; and it was followed by a *Boy Scout's Life of Lincoln* (1921). One of the most interesting is *A Reporter for Lincoln* (1927), an account of the experiences of a young soldier-reporter, Henry Wing, while on missions for the President.[19]

The book which best epitomizes her contribution to Lincoln literature, however, is *In the Footsteps of the Lincolns* (1924), which is essentially a reworking of the section of her Lincoln biography up to 1860. Before writing the book, Tarbell made a pilgrimage that began at Hingham, where Samuel Lincoln had begun the American family line, and that ended in Springfield. The journey functions as a frame for the history of the Lincoln family. *In the Footsteps of the Lincolns* is a distillation of its author's interpretation of Lincoln, as expressed in the poem by her editor and friend John Phillips. Phillips, who wrote the poem in 1908, caught to Tarbell's satisfaction the spirit of what she was trying to convey; for she used it as an epigraph:

Lincoln

In him distilled and potent the choice essence of a race!
Far back the Puritans—stern and manful visionaries,
Repressed poets, flushed with dreams of glowing theologies!
Each new succession, out of border hardship,

Refined to human use the initial rigor of the breed,
Passing to the next the unconscious possession of a perfecting soul!
Each forest clearing gave something of neighborly grace,
The rude play of cabin-bred natural people something of humor,
Each mountain home something of inner daring,
Each long-wandering life something of patience and of hope!
In the open, far-seen nature gradually chiseled
The deepening wistful eyes.
Each axman and each plowman added
Another filament of ruggedness;
Unknowing minds dumbly cried for liberty;
Mute hearts strove against injustice. . . .
At last was ready the alembic, where Nature stored and set apart
Each generation's finest residue,
Waiting for the hour of perfect mixture—
And then the Miracle!

Tarbell's explanation for Lincoln's rise was less poetic but just as Puritan. "Great mental and moral qualities, rigorously trained and kept steadily at work, brought Abraham Lincoln naturally into the Presidency of the United States," she declared in her preface. The key word is "naturally," for her whole point was to show that the "miracle" cited in Phillips's poem was not the result of sudden divine intervention but a predictable outcome of the racial stock that had produced Abraham Lincoln and the long succession of frontier experiences which had shaped his forbears and him.

In the Footsteps of the Lincolns, a very readable book, emphasizes Tarbell's strong points as a writer—her feeling for place, for personalities, her easy anecdotal style; and her invariably reverent tone is her chief flaw. The reviewers, who were generally favorable, stressed the book's merit as the first connected history of the Lincoln family, its placement of Lincoln in the mainstream of American experience, and its removing him from the stagnant backwater of a wilderness hovel. But the revaluation of the past taking place during the 1920's did not allow Tarbell's work to go unchallenged. Comments by Isabel Paterson, who reviewed *In the Footsteps of the Lincolns* for the New York *Tribune,* were sharply critical of what she seemingly took to be Tarbell's attempt to reinstate, through Lincoln, the white, Anglo-Saxon, Protestant, middle-class values currently being satirized by Sinclair Lewis, H. L.

Mencken, and innumerable other writers. In her review Paterson declared that "I think Miss Tarbell in part defeats her object by an excess of zeal. She is too much the devotee, insisting upon a trivial perfection, a conformity to superficial standards, in the antecedents of Lincoln. A gentle but none the less fanatical partisan spirit imparts the flavor of sentimentality to her championship."[20]

Although "fanatical" is too strong a word, it does reveal the obeisance to conformity which often marks Tarbell's writing, makes it too smoothly bland, and causes her too often to ignore the depths which underlie appearances. The Lincolns were, after all, not on a camping trip on the prairie; they were scrabbling with no great success for their very subsistence. Possibly a defensiveness before people from the urban East about her own beginnings caused Tarbell to overemphasize frontier respectability. Nevertheless, her great accomplishment remains her convincing demonstration that frontier folk were not debased castoffs living in backwoods slums who sporadically and inexplicably produced a genius capable of rising to the heights, but that they were an integral part of the whole society. Thus, she emphasized the continuity between the frontier and the rest of the country just as historian Frederick Jackson Turner, who was born in Wisconsin, had emphasized it. Turner's frontier thesis and Tarbell's revisionist account of Lincoln both arose in the 1890's as the finally settled West merged with the rest of the nation.

V   *Ida Tarbell as a Biographer*

Altogether, Ida Tarbell published five formal biographies. The first was that of Napoleon, including a short one of Josephine; although the biography of Madame Roland was written first, it was the second to be published. Her last two biographies were written toward the end of her career. The controversial *Life of Elbert H. Gary: The Story of Steel* was published in 1925; *Owen D. Young: A New Type of Industrial Leader* appeared in 1932, and was mistakenly taken for a campaign biography of Young, who was rumored at the time to be seeking the Democratic party's nomination for President. These last two biographies are discussed later in more detail, for they are more properly classified as business propaganda than as biography, since they are a study of a way of life that

Tarbell is defending. That way of life, outlined in those biographies previously considered, is the Anglo-American Protestant, antebellum way of the New England wing of the movement which erected in America the sole genuinely Protestant nation in history. Both the Napoleon and Roland biographies were antiaristocratic and antirevolutionary; and *Madame Roland* was, in addition, antifeminist. All favored a somewhat mystical egalitarianism harking back to the frontier, and an equally mystical evolutionism characteristic of the late nineteenth century.

Tarbell employed biography to point a moral and to teach a social lesson. She was not interested primarily in exploring her subjects' lives as individuals—only as types. Unless one accepts the validity of this approach and the validity of her world view, her biographies fail; for they are either condemnations of a society, as were her French biographies, or glorifications of one, as were those of Lincoln, Gary, and Young. Put in the simplified terms of a morality play, what begins to appear is an image of Eden, inhabited by a Lincolnian Adam, and an Eve more intent on begetting than balloting. With her next book, *The History of the Standard Oil Company*, a reptilian John D. Rockefeller slithers into view. That threat once disposed of, there would be no need to move east of Eden, for the white, Anglo-Saxon, Protestant Gary and Young represented the new Edenian order, one securely built on the foundations of the old.

Critics have tended to conclude that Tarbell sold out in her biographies of Gary and Young to the big business interests that she attacked in *The History of the Standard Oil Company*. She, however, found no inconsistency between the early work and the later ones; and she was correct, because her effort all along had been to find her way toward a synthesis of golden past and gilded present. Gary and Young can thus be considered legitimate offspring of the proprietors of her American Eden and not as the spawn of the serpent.

VI *New Directions*

By 1900, *McClure's Magazine* was an established success, partly because of McClure's vision and daring, partly because of brilliant execution of his schemes by the staff, and partly because of the exertions of Ida Tarbell, whose biographies caused gratifying rises in circulation and in the advertising revenue which accompanies it. Yet to the staff and to McClure something was lacking because the magazine had succeeded so far through imitation rather than through innovation. Frustrated and restless, they did not wish to have *McClure's* remain merely a livelier version of the *Century*. They were seeking an approach that would be both new and relevant to the times. Besides Ida Tarbell and John Phillips, the writing staff now included Ray Stannard Baker and Peter Finley Dunne, alter ego of "Mr. Dooley"; and it would soon include Lincoln Steffens.

During the Chicago World's Fair, McClure had sent Arthur Warren, another writer, to Chicago to write about the Armour Institute and its backer J. Ogden Armour, the head of the beef trust. This venture in turn inspired the idea for a series on great business achievements that was planned to begin around February, 1897. Trusts were much in the public eye but ignorance about their actual operations was widespread. As a result, said McClure, "the common people took a threatening attitude toward the trusts, and without much knowledge."[21] The project for the series on the trusts was dropped, but it was the germ for Ida Tarbell's *The History of the Standard Oil Company*, of Steffens's *The Shame of the Cities*, and of Baker's business-labor exposé *The Right to Work*. And *McClure's* thus became the originating force of the movement known as muckraking. The three series ran concurrently; they began with the first article in Tarbell's Standard Oil series in the November, 1902, issue of the magazine, and they continued until near the end of 1904.

McClure, who was quick to indicate what was transpiring, wrote in an editorial in the January, 1903, issue what remains the best short contemporary analysis from the Progressive point of view of the need for reform throughout the entire nation:

Concerning Three Articles in This Number of McClure's,
and a Coincidence that May Set Us Thinking

How many of those who have read through this number of the magazine noticed that it contains three articles on one subject? We did not plan it so; it is a coincidence that the January *McClure's* is such an arraignment of American character as should make every one of us stop and think. How many noticed that?

The leading article, "The Shame of Minneapolis," might have been called "The American Contempt of Law." That title could well have served for the current chapter of Miss Tarbell's History of Standard Oil. And it would have fitted perfectly Mr. Baker's "The Right to Work." All together, these articles come pretty near showing how universal is this dangerous trait of ours. Miss Tarbell has our capitalists conspiring among themselves, deliberately, shrewdly, upon legal advice, to break the law so far as it restrained them, and to misuse it to restrain others who were in their way. Mr. Baker shows labor, the ancient enemy of capital, and the chief complainant of the trust's unlawful acts, itself committing and excusing crimes. And in "The Shame of Minneapolis" we see the administration of a city employing criminals to commit crimes for the profit of elected officials, while the citizens—Americans of good stock and more than average culture, and honest, healthy Scandinavians—stood by complacent and not alarmed.

Capitalists, workingmen, politicians, citizens—all breaking the law, or letting it be broken. Who is left to uphold it? The Lawyers? Some of the best lawyers in the country are hired, not to go into court and defend cases, but to advise corporations and business firms how they can get around the law without too great a risk of punishment. The judges? Too many of them so respect the laws that for some "error" or quibble they restore to office or liberty men convicted on evidence overwhelmingly convincing to common sense. The churches? We know of one, an ancient and wealthy establishment, which had to be compelled by a Tammany holdover health officer to put its tenements in sanitary condition. The colleges? They do not understand.

There is no one left; none but all of us. Capital is learning (with indignation at labor's unlawful acts) that its rival's contempt for law is a menace to property. Labor has shrieked the belief that the illegal power of capital is a menace to the worker. These two are drawing together. Last November when a strike was threatened by the yard-men on all the railroads centering in Chicago, the men got together and settled by raising wages, and raising freight rates too. They made the public pay. The public is the people. We forget that we all are the people; that while each of us in his group can shove off on the rest the bill of today, the debt is only postponed; the rest are passing it back to us. We have to pay

in the end, every one of us. And in the end the sum total
of the debt will be our liberty.

Once more S. S. McClure's genius had prompted him to discern
the coincidence of market and mission. The exploitation of
that coincidence began one of the greatest eras in magazine
history.

CHAPTER 4

The History of the Standard Oil Company

A S befits an epic, *The History of the Standard Oil Company* begins *in medias res* at the pivotal moment when the Standard Oil Company, led by its thirty-three-year-old president, John D. Rockefeller, wrested control of the Pennsylvania Oil Regions from the original developers. With a deft, sure touch Tarbell evokes in her opening paragraph the frontier spirit which in her youth had dominated the region as it came to dominate her book:

One of the busiest corners of the globe at the opening of the year 1872 was a strip of Northwestern Pennsylvania, not over fifty miles long, known the world over as the Oil Regions. Twelve years before this strip of land had been but little better than a wilderness; its chief inhabitants the lumbermen, who every season cut green swaths of primeval pine and hemlock from its hills, and in the spring floated them down the Allegheny River to Pittsburgh. The great tides of Western emigration had shunned the spot for years as too rugged and unfriendly for settlement, and yet in twelve years this region avoided by men had been transformed into a bustling trade centre, where towns elbowed each other for place, into which three great trunk railroads had built branches, and every foot of whose soil was fought for by capitalists. It was the discovery and development of a new product, petroleum, which had made this change from wilderness to market-place. This product in twelve years not only peopled a waste place on the earth, it had revolutionized the world's methods of illumination and added millions upon millions of dollars to the wealth of the United States.[1]

In following chapters Tarbell, focusing unremittingly on the personality and actions of John D. Rockefeller as adversary, presents her account of the swift conquest of the Oil Regions by the Standard Oil Company, a conquest largely completed by 1878. The result was an oil monopoly and the formation of the first and greatest trust combination. A few surviving independent operators resisted Standard Oil and continued

fighting the corporation for long years before legislation
enacted early in the twentieth century began to curb the trust
and to restore some measure of competition in the oil industry.
The tension which provides dramatic unity for *The History
of the Standard Oil Company* is, therefore, the unequal
struggle for control of the Oil Regions between a great corporation, a devastatingly efficient revolutionary development
in business management, and the easily disunited independent
operators whose frail solidarity was easily breached by their
single-minded opponents, personified by Rockefeller.

I *Ida Tarbell's Point of View*

Tarbell's history recounts the development of the oil industry from the early hawking of petroleum as a medicine
guaranteed to cure everything prayer couldn't to its eventual
use as a lubricant and fuel in internal combustion engines.
The narrative follows the rise of the Standard Oil Company
from its inception following the Civil War to the height of
its unchecked power at the turn of the century. Tarbell's tone,
a mixture of cold disdain and white-hot moral indignation controlled by excellent documentation and a facade of objectivity,
seemed to hit the right note. An enthralled public followed
her serial account in *McClure's* for two years as she tirelessly
communicated to tens of thousands of readers "a clear and
succinct notion of the processes by which a particular industry
passes from the control of the many to that of the few."[2] Tarbell
nowhere leaves much room for doubt that she is a partisan
of "the many."

The History of the Standard Oil Company first appeared
in *McClure's* as a seventeen-article series. The first series of
nine was published monthly from November, 1902, to July,
1903. The concluding series—which ran from December, 1903,
to April, 1904, at irregular intervals thereafter, and ended in
October, 1904—was immediately followed by book publication. The McClure, Phillips Publishing Company edition
was followed by one from the Macmillan Company.[3] Seen
as a whole in book form, the history is relatively short, five
hundred and fifty pages; in addition, however, there is an
appendix of three hundred and twenty-five pages, which contains transcripts of court testimony, official documents, letters,
and the like cited in the text, in lieu of conventional footnotes.

There are, in all, sixty-four documents, as well as an index.

Tarbell's bias is unmistakably revealed in the format of the published volumes. For example, both volumes contain as frontispieces unflattering portraits of John D. Rockefeller. These later headed a markedly hostile character sketch of him that Tarbell wrote for *McClure's*, which appeared in the issues of July and August, 1905. In the first portrait, which was taken following an illness during which Rockefeller lost all his hair, he is seated, hands relaxed and resting on the chair arms. His age at the time was sixty-five, but he looked older. Yet the portrait projects a feral power, perhaps enhanced by Rockefeller's complete hairlessness. Even seated, his body appears bulky and strong. The large, egg-bald head is erect; the pale eyes, cold and narrow, are accentuated by the unexpected absence of eyebrows. The nose is straight and finely modeled, with nostrils slightly flared. The mouth is a gash between nose and chin. The slight stoop of age does not detract from the impression of dominance and power.

The other portrait, which appeared in the second volume, is a reproduction of a sketch made the previous year. The skullcap Rockefeller by then wore to conceal his baldness gives him the appearance of an Anglo-Saxon Shylock; but the impression of massive power is there, despite the slight stoop forward of the head above the bull neck. There is no hint in either portrait of the fragile old gentleman who benevolently handed dimes to children, the familiar Rockefeller image in the 1920's.

Nor are the epigraphs Tarbell chose for the book calculated to win a reader's sympathy for Rockefeller. A bittersweet mingling of Emersonianism and social Darwinism, the Emerson quotation from "Self-Reliance" is the individualistic dictum that "an institution is the lengthened shadow of one man." How ironically Emerson's words are meant to be interpreted is indicated by the second quotation, taken from an address by John D. Rockefeller, Jr., to students at Brown University. "The American Beauty Rose," the younger Rockefeller had said, "can be produced in its splendor and fragrance only by sacrificing the early buds which grow up around it." The second quotation swiftly removes any ambiguity from the first as Tarbell's history unfolds and as her judgment of the Standard Oil Company emerges. To her, the issue is ultimately that of democracy versus tyranny, in a moral context. Based upon this issue, her book takes on the heroic proportions of a drama of good versus evil. The issue and its dramatic treatment are reminiscent of the pioneer study of the Standard Oil Company, Henry Demarest Lloyd's *Wealth Against Commonwealth*, published in 1894. But, whereas Lloyd's book had been a jeremiad, Tarbell's was a comparatively cool analysis; and her tone lent more credence to her accusations.

The History of the Standard Oil Company contains editorial judgments from which a reader can scarcely fail to derive inferences unfavorable to Rockefeller and his corporation. Consequently, S. S. McClure's claim that the book was unbiased seems disingenuous. "Miss Tarbell," he asserted in an editorial, "in her narrative has made no attempt to work on the emotions of her readers. She has asked no sympathy for the independent oil men. Her story has been what is pretended to be, a straight historical narrative backed by documents."[4] Tarbell pretended no such thing; nor would she subsequently have been declared "the Joan of Arc of the Oil Regions" had she done so. She had a thesis, and she interpreted her documents in the light of it. Giving full credit to Rockefeller and his organization for their intelligence and efficiency, which had transformed the structure of business, she maintained, and employed her documentation to demonstrate, that illegal rebates and drawbacks from the railroads were the principal cause of Standard's rise and continued dominance in the oil industry.[5] The resulting control of oil transportation meant control of the industry; and such control was illegal and immoral. Therefore, Tarbell reasoned, the monopoly achieved by the Standard Oil Company was illegal and immoral.

But human affairs persist in smashing through logical containment; thus, historians of the Standard Oil Company have differed over this central point of interpretation. No responsible writer has denied that rebates played a large part in the rise of Standard Oil, but opinion divides on the primacy of their role. Henry Demarest Lloyd and Ida Tarbell insist on that primacy; in opposition, Gilbert Holland Montague, an early scholarly investigator, and Allan Nevins, the noted contemporary historian, hold that organizational genius, implemented by efficiency of operations, was the principal reason for Standard's success. To them, rebates, while important, are the secondary results, so to speak, of efficiency seizing a legitimate advantage in the absence of effective governmental control of transportation rates.

Lloyd and Tarbell were journalists writing in the heat of battle; but Montague and Nevins, who wrote as academic historians uninvolved in the late-nineteenth-century struggle between the many and the few, viewed the struggle as an economic one, whereas to the former it was moral, because their standard for all things was the Golden Rule. Rebates meant to them special privilege; that violated the Golden Rule, and that was that. Conversely, preoccupied by economics, Montague ignores the Golden Rule; and Nevins seems oftentimes to consign it to the public relations department. All four writers agree, by and large, on the facts.

A reader must decide for himself whether the materialism of the academic historians provides a better basis for a history of Standard Oil than does the moral idealism of the journalist-historians. Perhaps the simplest way to assess them is to examine six of the most notorious incidents occurring during the rise of Standard Oil and the conclusions about them of the four writers mentioned.

II *Rise of an Empire*

A brief account of the rise of Standard Oil and its leader provides a perspective for these incidents. John D. Rockefeller's career is an illustration of the Horatio Alger rags to riches formula. Poor but honest, Rockefeller was born in 1839 in the farm country of Southwestern New York, just across the state line from Tarbell's birthplace. Born the previous year in Quincy, Massachusetts, was Henry Adams, the heir to the tradition of a great New England family which had included two Presidents and a member of a mercantile aristocracy soon to be pushed aside by the post–Civil War industrial oligarchy that Rockefeller helped create.

After the Rockefeller family emigrated to America from Germany in the 1720's, they intermarried with British settlers in New York of New England stock. John's mother, Eliza Davison, was of Scottish descent and of Calvinist persuasion. John, her oldest son, inherited her serenity of manner, piety, and iron will. His father, William Avery Rockefeller, had a checkered career, physical vitality, and buoyant charm. His mysterious and unexplained comings and goings gave rise to many local legends. It is believed that his main source of income came from the sale of patent medicines in the frontier areas of the Midwest.[6] His son John's career, equally mysterious and unexplained, soon gave rise to international legends when Standard Oil products began to light the lamps of China and all the world.

The family moved in 1853 to Cleveland, where John attended high school. His mother taught him piety and sobriety; his father, David Harum's advice: "Do unto others as they would do to you, and do it fust."[7] Thus equipped, John attended Folsom's Commercial College for three months in 1855, and was then hired as a bookkeeper-clerk by the firm of Hewitt and Tuttle, Cleveland produce merchants. Soon dissatisfied with his prospects, Rockefeller, now nineteen years old, invested his savings and some money borrowed from his father in a partnership with another ambitious young man, Maurice B. Clark, who was ten years his senior. Their business involved commission marketing of farm produce, and it prospered during the Civil War. Meanwhile, oil refineries had been established in Cleveland, a natural refining center on the western edge of the Oil Regions, situated on Lake Erie, and served by two major railroads.

The chief uses of oil at that time were for light and lubrication, but Rockefeller immediately grasped the great worldwide possibilities of oil marketing. By 1865, he was ready to stake his future in oil; by 1870, he realized that centralization and operational efficiency in all phases of the business were vital to survival in the highly competitive new industry; and he started organizing what soon became the Standard Oil Company. He and his associates, among them his brother William, had a capitalization of one million dollars when the decisive struggle began among the forces contending for control of the oil industry. The producers and refiners of the Oil Regions were determined to retain control of the industry they had literally built with their own bare hands. Arrayed against them were refiners in Cleveland, Pittsburgh, Philadelphia, and New York City; and they were the Johnny-come-latelys to the Pennsylvanians. These outsiders gradually consolidated with the Standard Oil Company, as with relentless aim, Standard absorbed its competitors. By 1878, the Standard Oil Company refined 90 to 95 percent of the total oil production of the United States which was still largely confined to the Pennsylvania oil fields. "Standard Oil" became an epithet of anathema in the Oil Regions, as did the name of Rockefeller. Standard Oil continued, nonetheless, to down rivals, extend its grip on pipelines and rail transport, and acquire fleets of its own tank cars. The company leased new oil lands and successfully sought control of marketing facilities. In 1882, the stock of Standard Oil was transferred into the Standard Oil Trust, the first of its kind.

Naturally, opposition to Standard's ruthlessly efficient business methods mounted as the remaining independent oil men saw the company's control tightened not only by means of efficient centralization but also through favorable freight rates against which competition became ruinous. Consequently, the company's history is glutted with records of court suits against it by individuals, states, and the federal government; with transcripts of legislative investigations; with criticisms of its brutal practices in the press; with lectures and public forums; and with magazine articles and books. Much of the alarm was aroused by the proliferation of other industrial trusts that emulated Standard's. By 1890, it was deemed necessary to enact the regulatory Sherman Anti-Trust Act.[8]

In 1892, the Ohio charter of the Standard Oil Company was revoked by the Ohio Supreme Court under the provisions of the Sherman Anti-Trust Act. Standard Oil nullified the decison through time-consuming legal moves and other stalling tactics until 1898, when the State of Ohio sued the company for contempt of court. Standard Oil evaded the suit by incorporating in New Jersey, which became known as "the Mother of Trusts" because it provided increasing numbers of harried trusts a home away from home with its liberal charter provisions and with few questions asked. When Standard Oil and twenty constituent companies forthwith merged their stock, the company became possibly the richest holding company in the world.

Even as Ida Tarbell marshaled public opinion against the practices of Standard Oil, the federal government was moving in the direction of yet another suit against the company, one which culminated in 1911 with a United States Supreme Court decision that dissolved the Standard Oil Trust. *The History of the Standard Oil Company* was thus a journalist's articulation of the public's opposition to the trusts and, at the same time, a powerful agent in hastening the legal solution of the trust problem. Following the Supreme Court decision of 1911, Tarbell became a supporter of big business; for it was not big business itself to which she objected but special privilege. Once convinced that this abuse was satisfactorily curbed, she ceased her attack. A true conservative, her main drive was to uphold the ideological *status quo ante bellum;* and S. S. McClure spoke for her, as well as for himself, when he recorded in his autobiography:

When I came to this country, an immigrant boy, in 1866, I believed the government of the United States was the flower of all the ages—that nothing could possibly corrupt it. It seemed the one of all human institutions that could not come to harm. This feeling was general, at home and abroad. The nation had, during the Civil War, risen to moral heights which it has never since attained. The war itself resulted in opening easy avenues of corruption. During the struggle, and for years before, everything else had been neglected for the one great question of slavery. People felt that if this were righted, nothing could be wrong. The great resources of the continent were rapidly opening up, with no provision being made to control them, or to control the few able men who were bound to seize and utilize these unparalleled resources for their own ends. . . . The American people went on believing that they were still what they once had been, but they were not. . . . I would like to do my part to help bring about the realization of the very noble American Ideal, which, when I was a boy, was universally believed in, here and in Europe.[9]

If McClure's view is utopian, Americans in those days were born utopians.

III   *Tales from the American Jungle*

If Henry Demarest Lloyd originated the dramatic structure which was to characterize studies of the Standard Oil Company's rise, Tarbell refined it by banking the flames of the Lloyd rhetoric. The cast of characters remained the same; Rockefeller (never named in Lloyd's account) was assigned the role of Greed; and the independents became Faith, Hope, and Charity. Lloyd's *Wealth Against Commonwealth* had been an exposé that had revealed the company as an "Anaconda," squeezing the life out of free enterprise through criminal collusion; exploitation of helpless independents or, worse, of their widows; sabotage, espionage, illegal control of oil transportation; and political corruption. All charges were documented, but the use made of the documents became the issue.

For example, Ida Tarbell criticized, on philosophical grounds, *The Rise and Progress of the Standard Oil Company*, a monograph written by Montague while he was a Ricardo Scholar in economics at Harvard, and published in 1903 by Harper's while Tarbell's series was appearing in *McClure's*. It was widely believed that publication of Montague's study, far from being coincidental, had in fact been subsidized by the Standard Oil Company, since the study justified the activities of the company on purely economic grounds. Tarbell, still indignant decades later, tartly recalled that Montague had "separated business and ethics in a way that must have been a comfort to 26 Broadway," Standard's New York headquarters.[10] The young Ricardo Scholar, stung by the rough handling his published study had received, attacked Tarbell's historiography as myth-making in a disdainful article which appeared in the *North American Review*.

Tarbell had begun the first chapter of *The History of the Standard Oil Company* with a lyrical sketch of a sylvan paradise inhabited by innocent industry. The chapter ended with paradise lost, as the Standard Oil Company and its allies attempted a take-over:

Life ran swift and ruddy and joyous in these men [of the Oil Regions]. They were still young, most of them under forty, and they looked forward with all the eagerness of the young who have just learned of their powers, to years of struggle and development. They would solve all [their] perplexing problems of over-production, of railroad discrimination, of speculation. . . . They would meet their own needs. They would bring the oil refining to the region where it belonged. They would make their towns the most beautiful in the world. There was nothing too good for them, nothing they did not hope and dare. But suddenly, at the heyday of this confidence, a big hand reached out from nobody knew where, to steal their conquest and throttle their future. The suddenness and the blackness of the assault on their business stirred to the bottom their manhood and sense of fair play, and the whole region arose in a revolt which is scarcely paralleled in the commercial history of the United States.[11]

The "big hand" was that of the South Improvement Company, a conspiratorial combination of railroads and oil refiners whose

unavowed purpose was the restraint of trade. The hand reached
out from Cleveland, Pittsburgh, and Philadelphia refineries;
from the headquarters of the Pennsylvania, the Erie, and the
New York Central railroads. The wall of resistance hastily
erected by the Pennsylvania independents contained, for the
moment, the assault; but the hand inscribed indelible writing
thereon.

IV *The South Improvement Company Scheme*

In 1871, a shift of production southward to newly discovered
fields in the Oil Regions threatened the business of the New
York Central and the Erie railroads and favored the Pennsylvania Railroad, which already had lines in the area. The other
two lines supplied Cleveland refineries with crude oil; that
city was suffering from competition and from dipping profits
resulting from overproduction in the rich new fields, as were
refiners in other large cities that ringed the region. The situation was serious. To remedy it, according to Montague, "a
combination of the railroads and refiners was planned. 'It had
its inception,' to quote ... the editor of the *Oil City Derrick,*
'with certain Philadelphia and Pittsburgh refiners, with an
agreement for co-operation with certain Cleveland refiners.
But philosophical minds ... are agreed that it had its origin,
as a matter of fact, with the railroad interests rather than the
oil interests.' The form which this combination took," Montague resumed, "was a contract between the railroads and certain refiners of Pittsburgh, Philadelphia, and Cleveland organized into the South Improvement Company."[12]

On May 1, 1871, the Pennsylvania legislature conferred upon
the South Improvement Company certain powers that had
been granted exclusively by it the previous year to the Pennsylvania Railroad. The powers, as broad as they were indefinite,
included the authority to construct any facilities needed to
increase land or water traffic anywhere in the United States.
There were a total of two thousand shares in the company,
and nine hundred of these were owned by H. M. Flagler,
O. H. Payne, William Rockefeller, H. Bostwick, and J. D.
Rockefeller, all of the Standard Oil Company of Cleveland.
The intent of the contract between the railroads and the refiners
was to divide traffic among the three competing railroads. The

refiners agreed to ship 45 percent of their oil over the Pennsylvania line, to split shipments of the remainder evenly between the other two, to furnish tankage facilities and tank cars, and to keep records of all oil shipments "both by itself and by other parties."[13] The "other parties" were, of course, competitors. The South Improvement Company was to receive rebates from the railroads on all petroleum and its products transported, including those of its competitors.

In addition, the railroads promised to charge competitors of the South Improvement Company full freight rates, as specified in their contract with that company. That rate was approximately double the then current one. This contract was a deadly missile armed to destroy competition, and its implications understandably spread fear and outrage across the Oil Regions when news of it had leaked out. In the face of that outrage, the railroads' assurance that similar arrangements would be made with any company which could ship as much oil as the South Improvement Company, as well as provide equal shipping facilities, sounds hollow, no matter how fair it may look on paper. In effect, the refiners of the combination were to act as "eveners" for the railroads, guaranteeing their survival by eliminating the ruinous freight wars among them. Inevitably, the refiners of the South Improvement Company would quickly acquire every refinery in sight by manipulating at will the price of crude oil. The efficiency of such a scheme is obvious, however doubtful its morality may be.

Montague stresses, as does Nevins, that such contracts were part of railroad policy at that time, and were routinely entered into with cattle and grain shippers, as well as with oil men. "Such are the economic grounds," concluded Montague, on which to base judgment of the South Improvement Company scheme. "Popular judgment, however," he added, "was much less deliberate." (Montague's circumlocution refers to the riots and embargoes on oil shipments by independents which forced the abrogation of the contract, under which not a single barrel of oil was ever actually shipped.) "From the railway point of view," he continued, ... "the situation in 1872 justified a special contract; and in the South Improvement Company was presented the fittest party to such a contract."[14]

Nevertheless, Montague decided the scheme had been a mistake.

Whether the rebate provided by the contract excessively rewarded the company for its services as "evener" is a question of fact, not to be settled offhand. The violent popular uprising, the quickness with which the contract was withdrawn by the railroads, and the reticence and subsequent penitence of all concerned in making it, and the odium in which it has since been held by both friends and enemies of the Standard Oil Company may indeed be regarded as evidence that its provisions were unwarranted. The principle of the contract, however—the combination of both railways and the strongest refiners to restore profitable stability to traffic and industry—was inevitable in the practice and theory of railway economics.[15]

What Montague apparently meant is that the principle was applied in an unprincipled manner.

Nevins seems to have believed that the principle was applied in total ignorance of the importance of good public relations to business. Writing from the perspective of the 1950's, he stated coolly:

Our dispassionate conclusion, finally, must be that while something can be said in defense of a refiners' combination to stabilize oil-prices and "even" oil shipments, this particular scheme was both defective and dangerous. It took inadequate account of the well-owners and consumers. Its weapon against stubborn independents was brutal and indefensible. Its sponsors never furnished convincing proof that they were working for an individual association and not a small ring. Rockefeller's adherence to the plan for tactical reasons can be understood; but his participation in it was highly unfortunate for his business reputation. In the Regions especially it left a black mark of discredit and suspicion against his name. He should have stayed entirely clear of so hasty, ill-organized, and potentially tyrannical an organization. His participation suggests, as do numerous episodes in his later career—that he had an inadequate understanding of popular psychology, and an inadequate appreciation of the fact that in the last analysis business must work within the rules imposed by public opinion.[16]

Far from treating the scheme as merely an unfortunate tactical blunder, Lloyd and Tarbell maintained that the motivation behind it controlled the subsequent history of the Standard Oil Company. "There has never been any real break in the plans revealed 'partly born, and buried' in 1872," Lloyd accused. "From then until now, in 1893, every fact that has come to the surface has shown them in full career. If they were buried, it was as seed is—for a larger crop of the same thing."[17] That Tarbell agreed is evident throughout *The History of the Standard Oil Company,* and in her concluding chapter she specifically reiterates it:

Few men in either the political or industrial life of this country can point to an achievement carried out in more exact accord with its first conception than John D. Rockefeller, for both in purpose and methods the Standard Oil Company has always been the form of the South Improvement Company, by which Mr. Rockefeller first attracted general attention in the oil industry. The original scheme has suffered many modifications. Its most offensive feature, the drawback on other people's shipments, has been cut off. Nevertheless, to-day, as at the start, the purpose of the Standard Oil Company is the purpose of the South Improvement Company—the regulation of the price of crude and refined oil by the control of output; and the chief means for sustaining this purpose is still that of the original scheme—a control of oil transportation giving special privileges in rates.[18]

The role of rebates was central, therefore, in the creation of the Standard monopoly. Montague and Nevins explain them as unavoidable, given the economic condition of the oil industry at the time. Nevins was critical regarding Tarbell's minimizing of the desperate straits to which unbridled competition of the independents had brought the industry.[19] Tarbell and Lloyd contend, however, that rebates were clearly contrary to common law regarding public transportation and that therefore discrimination in rates was *ipso facto* immoral. Referring to the men of the Oil Regions, Tarbell declared that "they believed in independent effort—every man for himself and fair play for all. They wanted competition, loved open fight. They considered all business should be done openly; that the railways were bound as public carriers to give equal rates; that any combination which favored one firm or one locality at the expense of another was illegal. This belief long held by many of the oil men had been crystallized by the uprising [against the South Improvement Company] into a common sentiment. It had become the moral code of the region."[20]

Tarbell's and Lloyd's accounts contain the perhaps exaggerated moral idealism of the Old America, and the academicians' separation of business and ethics is perhaps a bit self-consciously tough-minded and "scientific."

V *The Widow's Tale*

The second infamous incident in the rise of the Standard Oil Company concerns, not collusion and conspiracy aimed at independent oil operators, but the alleged mulcting of a Cleveland widow whose refinery, her sole source of support, was acquired by John D. Rockefeller. Lloyd, followed by Ida Tarbell, used the experience of Mrs. F. M. Backus, the widow of a Cleveland refiner, to illustrate the ruthless means that Rockefeller employed to build his empire. Although Lloyd had uncritically accepted the merits of the widow's case, Tarbell was more cautious; she included in her account Rockefeller's statement in defense of his actions, and conceded in a rare footnote that his statements were supported by others connected with the sale of the Backus refinery.[21] Tarbell's purpose in citing the incident was not, as Lloyd's had been, to accuse Rockefeller of despicably cheating a helpless widow who was the sole support of her children. Rather, she sought to demonstrate through the widow's heartrending difficulties the fear that Rockefeller inspired in the independents whose businesses he coveted, a fear which made "refusal to sell" impossible.[22]

Fred M. Backus, one of the earliest oil refiners in Cleveland, had gone into the business in 1860, the year following the Drake discovery; and his main product was lubricating oil. At the time of the sale to Rockefeller, Standard Oil refined and marketed only illuminating oil, pursuant to an agreement with Backus that he sell them his oil suitable for lamps; in return, Standard had agreed to stay out of the lubricating oil end of the business. This was the situation in 1874, when Backus died. Court records contain the rest of the story.

According to Mrs. Backus, her husband had died in debt. She carried on the business for the sake of her "fatherless children," earning "handsome profits" thereby. In November, 1878, an agent of Standard Oil approached her about the possibility of selling the business. She refused to deal with him, requesting to see John D. Rockefeller himself. A few days later Rockefeller obligingly appeared. "I told Mr. Rockefeller," reported the Widow Backus, "that I realized the fact that the

B[ackus] Oil Company was entirely in the power of the Standard Oil Company, and that all I could do would be to appeal to his honor as a gentleman and his sympathy to do with me the best that he could."[23] Rockefeller, she testified, had reacted sympathetically to her plight; and he had promised "with tears in his eyes" to deal fairly with her during sale negotiations. He also promised that she could retain any amount of stock she chose in her company, short of a controlling majority. Where Mrs. Backus quoted a sale price of two hundred thousand dollars, Standard Oil "ridiculed" the amount, said the widow; it countered with an offer of seventy-nine thousand dollars and demanded that each stockholder in the Backus Oil Company provide a bonded guarantee to refrain from engaging in the oil business for ten years after the sale was completed.

Reconciled to the necessity for selling at Standard's price, Mrs. Backus requested that she be allowed to retain fifteen thousand dollars' worth of her stock. But, when the Standard negotiators refused, she was hurried into parting with stock and refinery. She then had second thoughts and sent a letter to Rockefeller threatening to publicize details of the deal. In a return letter Rockefeller stated that he would give her back the whole works and cancel the deal, if she wished, or she could retain the stock she had requested. But, in the meantime, Mrs. Backus, once more changing her mind, had agreed to the deal on the negotiators' terms and had sold out completely. Mrs. Backus became "so indignant" about Rockefeller's belated reply that she "threw the letter into the fire and paid no further attention to it."[24]

Rockefeller, less impetuous in the disposition of correspondence than Mrs. Backus appears to have been, kept a copy of his reply to her letter, which appeared in his affidavit. In the letter he assured her that he had thoroughly reviewed the deal to make certain that she had been fairly treated. It had been his understanding, he wrote, that she had decided to sell out completely; and he complained that her letter did him "grievous wrong." For after all, he remarked, "it was of but little moment to the interests represented by me whether the business of the B[ackus] Oil Company was purchased or not."[25] Furthermore, he reminded her, she had offered to sell out to Standard two years before "at considerably less

price." He continued that the sixty thousand dollars offered
for her property was at least three times its replacement cost.
He gave her three days to reach a decision.[26] We have seen
what the Widow Backus thought of his offer.

Lloyd's report of the troubles of the Widow Backus is too
biased to be reliable. Tarbell's presents both sides, her point
being that "where there's smoke there's fire." If the widow's
tale gained wide credence, which it had, Tarbell reasoned
that it must conform to a pattern typical of Standard's methods.
In a hostile review of *The History of the Standard Oil Company,* Gilbert Holland Montague commented that the affidavits
ranged against Mrs. Backus's statement of her case outnum-
bered hers three to one and that these were from her own
company's associates, a fact that he claimed Tarbell unduly
deemphasized.[27] Nevins also points to the affidavits countering
Mrs. Backus's statement, and he considers her complaints
baseless. What's more, according to his account, "this 'poor
widow' conserved her money shrewdly and according to
Clevelanders died worth about $300,000."[28]

Does Tarbell load her account of the widow's travails with
unfair innuendo? Does Nevins, on the other hand, too blandly
gloss over the sanction of force Standard wielded, a sanction
so absolute that the company was able to seize any properties
it desired, at unfair prices, with all parties to the sales smil-
ing—on the outside, at any rate—except the Widow Backus?
Was the story folklore Tarbell skillfully used for propaganda,
as Montague implied? Certainly, the tale of the Widow Backus
demonstrates that, even among historians, one man's fact is
all too often another's folklore.

The importance of the South Improvement Company
episode and the Backus case to Rockefeller himself is evidenced by his vigorous defense of his dealings with the Widow
Backus and by his justification of rebates. These appeared
in his book *Random Reminiscences of Men and Events,* published in 1909. In it he declared his intention to set the record
straight about incidents in the history of the Standard Oil Company which had not been "fully understood" by the public.
In his discussion of the Backus affair he cited the same
affidavits against the Widow Backus that Nevins later used
in Rockefeller's defense. He ended his account with genuine
puzzlement, still apparently bewildered by her unpredictable

impetuosity: "So far as I can see, after more than thirty years have elapsed, there was nothing but the most kindly and considerate treatment of Mrs. Backus on the part of the Standard Oil Company. I regret that Mrs. Backus did not take at least a part of her pay in Standard certificates, as we suggested she should do."[29] This regret may well have been shared by her, for she would have become a millionaire had she done so.

On the topic of rebates Rockefeller was flatly pragmatic. He explained that, of course, Standard received rebates, as that had been "the railroads' method of business." Furthermore, he continued, the custom conformed to "the natural laws of trade." Then shifting the pea under another shell, he asserted that "the profits of the Standard Oil Company did not come from advantages given by railroads. The railroads, rather, were the ones who profited by the Standard Oil Company."[30] With impish amusement he concluded his defense of rebates with a remark made by "a bright man from Boston" about them: "I am opposed on principle to the whole system of rebates and drawbacks—unless I am in on it."[31]

VI *The March to the Sea:*
Standard and the Seaboard Pipelines

The third incident during the ongoing commercial warfare between the Standard Oil Company and the independent oil operators took place on the technological front. Standard's role in the development of pipelines exemplified a common complaint about the company: it would allow independents to take risks in perfecting and testing technological innovations and then appropriate them, leaving crumbs of the profits for their originators, or none, as the case might be. The story of the take-over of the Tidewater Pipeline Company is a classic instance.

In 1876 a group of independents in the Oil Regions became excited over a plan suggested by the Seaboard Pipe Line Company to construct a pipeline from the Oil Regions to Baltimore, a feat theretofore deemed impossible; but Seaboard failed and went into receivership. Two years later the plan was revived by the newly organized Tidewater Pipe Line Company, and the right of way to Baltimore from the Bradford oil fields in Pennsylvania was quietly secured. In addition, the new plans

included pipelines to New York refineries which would permit
the independents to bypass Standard's virtual control of transportation. A line one hundred and nine miles long was laid
to Williamsport, Pennsylvania, a point east of the previously
impassable Allegheny Mountains; and from there the oil was
to be temporarily carried to New York and Philadelphia by
the Reading Railroad, a newcomer to oil transportation.

By the spring of 1879, all was ready for the test of the line
to Williamsport, despite opposition from Standard and the railroads. The successful trial was watched with mounting excitement. Soon after, when Tidewater had completed its pipeline
to New York, transportation costs were significantly lower than
those of rail transport. The end of railroad control of long distance oil transporation was at hand, but this stunning
technological triumph was a serious threat to the Standard
Oil Company, and Rockefeller and his associates reacted
swiftly. Focusing as usual on Rockefeller, Tarbell reported
that "a man of lesser intellect might not have foreseen the
inevitableness of the new situation; a man of lesser courage
would not have sprung to meet it. Mr. Rockefeller, however,
is like all great generals; he never fails to foresee where the
battle is to be fought; he never fails to get the choice of positions. He wasted no time in deciding what should be done.
He proposed not merely to control future long-distance oil
transportation; he proposed to own it."[32]

Consequently, in 1883, the year following Standard's organization as the original trust company, a Standard subsidiary,
the National Transit Company, merged with the Tidewater
Pipe Line Company, which was allocated 11.5 percent of the
oil traffic passing through the pipelines it had built. Since
Standard's subsidiary kept the rest, Standard kept control of
the price of oil.[33] Practically speaking, the Standard Oil Company was forced to overcome the threat of the pipeline company or lose its dominance. In Tarbell's account of the episode,
she awards full credit to the Standard men for the brilliance
of the counterattack. Basically her objection is that, beyond
a point, bigness in an institution is stultifying; that a huge
industrial complex is characterized by conventional, unin-
spired thinking because it is simply too cumbersome; and that
it is tied down by too many interests to chance the daring
originality which results in technological progress. Instead,
such a giant is limited to the negative role of "spoiler."

Tarbell also pointed to the episode as additional evidence for the contention that, left to themselves, the independents of the Oil Regions could have developed the industry without the intervention of Standard's vaunted efficiency; for competition is the mother of invention, as in the case of Tidewater's ingenious exploitation of a new concept in transportation. Lloyd, Montague, and Nevins responded to the Tidewater incident in predictable ways. Lloyd, concerned about the consumers' interests, loudly squawked *"FOUL!"* Montague described the incident with neither praise nor condemnation. Nevins regarded it as one more demonstration that a good big man can always whip a good little man.[34]

CHAPTER *5*

The History of the
Standard Oil Company,
Continued

THE following three episodes in Standard Oil history occurred in the 1880's and were used to support
Tarbell's thesis that the methods employed in the abortive
South Improvement Company scheme continued to characterize those of the Standard Oil Company. The first incident
concerns the long battle of an Ohio independent oil man
against the industrial colossus; the second, a notorious case
of alleged industrial sabotage by a Standard subsidiary; and
the third, legislative investigations of charges of political corruption brought against the Standard Oil Company.

I *George Rice versus the Standard Oil Company*

The prolonged legal warfare between George Rice, independent producer-refiner of Marietta, Ohio, and the most powerful
corporation in the world represented in the public's mind a
drama in which George, while never able to slay the dragon,
did manage to fight it off. Rice was embroiled in continuous
litigation from the 1870's to the 1890's against Standard Oil
that usually involved the company's marketing or transportation tactics against him as a competitor. Though Rice often
lost in the law courts, he rarely lost in the court of public
opinion. In Tarbell's discussion of a series of cases involving
Standard's punitive use of rebates against competitors, including those of the redoubtable Rice, she notes Rockefeller's
obtuseness concerning public opinion that was to prove to
be his Achilles' heel.

Espionage was a main source of Standard's uncanny knowledge of rivals' shipments, she declared; and, though there
was, she continued, "certainly . . . nothing of the transcenden-

78

tal in this kind of omniscience," it nevertheless inspired a superstitious fear among competitors and the general public, a fear which inevitably generated a reaction:

If Mr. Rockefeller had been as great a psychologist as he is a business manipulator he would have realized that he was awakening a terrible popular dread, and he would have foreseen that one day, with the inevitable coming to light of his methods, there would spring up about his name a crop of scorn which would choke any crop of dollars and donations which the wealth of the earth could produce. The effect of this dread was deplorable, for it intensified the feeling that it was useless to make further effort at combined resistance. And yet these men, who were now lying too supine in Mr. Rockefeller's steel glove even to squirm, had laid the foundations of freedom in the oil business. It has taken thirty years to demonstrate the inestimable value of the efforts which in 1884 they regarded as futile—thirty years to build even a small structure on the foundation, though that much has been done.[1]

George Rice was one of the outstanding squirmers. His most notorious suit involved rebates and drawbacks on his oil shipments by the Standard Oil Company. Rice brought suit in 1885 and won his case. In 1883, Rice began to refine oil from his wells in the Macksburg field of Southeastern Ohio, near Marietta. The crude was shipped by the Cincinnati and Marietta Railroad, which granted Rice a rebate for the use of his own tank car. Before long Standard Oil arrived in the Macksburg field; and it arranged not only for a rebate on its oil but also for drawbacks on that of its rivals in the field.

After anxious consultation with his attorneys, General Phineas Pease, receiver in charge of the bankrupt Cincinnati and Marietta Railroad, consented to the arrangement. On March 20, 1885 (thirteen years after the discovery and disavowal of the South Improvement Company scheme), the arrangement went into effect. Rice promptly built a short pipeline to the Muskingum River so he could ship his oil by barge to his Marietta refinery. In the spring, however, before completion of the pipeline, he had shipped 1,360 barrels of oil by rail, for which Standard Oil had received a three-hundred-and-forty-dollar drawback. In due time the Standard Oil Company refunded the money to Rice. But the transaction had meanwhile come to the notice of the judge reviewing

General Pease's stewardship, and he deemed it deficient. He fired Pease and referred the case to a master commissioner for further probing. The master found that twelve days *after* the judge had ordered Pease to bring his freight contracts to court, Rice's money had been returned.[2]

The Rice case created a sensation. John D. Rockefeller violated his vow of silence and granted an interview to the New York *World* on March 29, 1890. His defense was reasonable and mildly worded: "When the arrangement was reported to the offices of the company at New York, it was not agreed to because our counsel pronounced it illegal. . . . We repudiated the contract before it was passed on by the courts and made full recompense. In a business as large as ours, conducted by so many agents, some things are likely to be done which we cannot approve of. We correct them as soon as they come to our knowledge. The public hears of the wrong—it never hears of the correction."[3]

Montague referred to the Rice case, which he called "indefensible," in *The Rise and Progress of the Standard Oil Company*. Noting that the drawback money was refunded "before the suit was brought to remove the receiver," he dismissed the incident as untypical of Standard's methods following the formation of the trust.[4] Lloyd focused on Rice's independence and courage in building his own pipeline to offset Standard Oil's machinations. Nevins, who termed the arrangement "outrageous," placed the blame for it on the "reckless and unscrupulous" Daniel O'Day, a subordinate Standard Oil Company officer; and he concluded that "history must censure the Standard for inexcusable negligence." Still, he continued, echoing Montague's judgment, the episode was "untypical; nobody ever seriously asserted after 1881 that Standard made a *practice* of demanding drawbacks upon competitive shipments."[5] Tarbell used the Rice incident to pound home her theory that Standard Oil continued throughout its history to carry out the aims of the South Improvement Company in order to destroy by any means all competition in the industry. The question remains: Was the money returned to Rice *because* suit was brought, or was it returned in the normal order of business?

II *The Buffalo Oil Company Case*

Another link in the chain of evidence against Standard Oil

was the notorious case of the Buffalo Oil Company of New York *versus* the Vacuum Oil Company of Rochester, New York, a Standard subsidiary. The case struck the vital center of the Standard Oil Company; for three top officials—H. H. Rogers, John Archbold, and Ambrose McGregor, also board members of Vacuum Oil—were accused of criminal conspiracy to sabotage the Buffalo Oil Works and were indicted. Although the indictment was subsequently dropped for lack of evidence, the fact of it was extremely damaging. As in the Rice case, the lawsuit apparently came as a profound shock to the top men of Standard that they were held by the public, and the courts, as personally accountable for mishaps which occurred throughout their vast empire.

With an eye on libel laws, Tarbell began her account of the case with a carefully worded introductory passage:

Very soon after Mr. Rockefeller began to "acquire" independent refineries, whose owners were loath to sell or go out of business, unpleasant stories began to be circulated in the oil world of the methods used in getting the offending plants out of the way. When freight discriminations, cutting off crude supply, and price wars in the market failed, other means were tried, and these means included, it was whispered, the actual destruction of the plants. The only case in which this charge was made which ever came to trial was that of the Buffalo Lubricating Oil Company, Limited.[6]

In 1880, J. Scott Wilson, a salesman for the Vacuum Oil Company, quit to go into business for himself. He took with him another salesman for the company, Charles B. Matthews. They formed a company and decided to build a refinery in Buffalo. The two salesmen planned to construct an already patented vacuum still because they were certain that they could prove the patents invalid. Indeed, Matthews assured Wilson, who evidently was hesitant, that Vacuum probably would be willing to settle out of court for a hundred thousand dollars to prevent the use of their distilling process rather than prosecute. That remark was to cost Matthews in the future, for Standard Oil seized upon it as evidence of intent to blackmail the company by forcing it to buy him and Wilson out.

Since both men were salesmen, they needed an experienced stillman to supervise plant operations. They found their man in another Vacuum employee, Albert Miller. Sensing money to be made in the bold new venture, Miller joined the company in 1881. He then had some parts used in Vacuum Company stills cast at a foundry, not denying the foundryman's impression that the parts were intended for Vacuum.

The owners of the Vacuum Oil Company, Hiram B. Everest and his son Charles, had sold out to Standard in 1879, retaining a quarter interest in the business and continuing to run it. The younger Everest was in charge when he was informed of the desertion of his former employees. He immediately and forcefully told them he would do everything he could to ruin their business. When he tried to lure Miller back with a promise of a twenty-thousand-dollar "bonus," Miller stood firm. Aware that Miller was the weak link in the Buffalo concern, the Everests continued to work on him. Miller began to neglect his work and became a chronic absentee. Soon he professed himself willing to sabotage the Buffalo Oil Company's first run of oil. In mid-June, when one of the company's stills was ready to go, Miller ordered an extremely hot fire to be put under it to hasten distillation. The safety valve finally blew off the still, releasing clouds of heavy yellow vapor. Miller readjusted the valve, once more calling for an extremely hot fire beneath the still. Again the valve blew, with alarming results. There were fortunately no injuries, and no fire resulted, but a hundred and seventy-five barrels of oil were ruined.

A week later Miller fled Buffalo to meet the senior Everest in New York. He telegraphed his wife to move from Buffalo to Rochester, and to take the furniture so Matthews could not attach it. Miller then embarked on a series of moves to hide himself from his former associates in Buffalo. Eventually he was put on a retainer of fifteen hundred dollars a year by the Everests and consigned to California. The Everests then forced Wilson to leave the Buffalo firm by filing a suit claiming that his leaving Vacuum had been unlawful. The suit was settled out of court, and Wilson left the firm. Matthews was in trouble without his stillman and salesman. When Vacuum filed suit against him for infringement of its patent, he knew that, with Standard's backing, the company could afford to continue such suits indefinitely. When Matthews then offered to sell his company to Standard Oil for a hundred thousand dollars, the offer was refused.

Vacuum Oil now bombarded Matthews with patent suits. He lost one, but he was ordered to pay a mere six cents damage to Vacuum instead of the twelve thousand dollars it had demanded. However, Matthews was plagued by litigation which was draining his capital. In turn, he sued his tormentors for one hundred thousand dollars for harassment. In the meantime, he learned that the elusive Albert Miller had returned to Rochester and was through with the Everests. Albert Miller now believed that he had both Vacuum and Standard literally "over a barrel," and he threatened to reveal Vacuum schemes to sabotage the Buffalo Oil Company works unless he was paid off by them. Matthews promptly got in touch with Albert. In March, 1885, five years after the inception of his company, the jury in his civil suit against the Everests awarded Matthews twenty thousand dollars of the hundred-thousand-dollar damages he had asked. The judge hearing the case cut the award to four thousand dollars.

Once more the litigious Matthews brought suit, for he was convinced that Albert Miller's story of being incited to ruin the Buffalo Oil Company's first run of oil would increase his award of damages. In the new civil suit Matthews demanded two hundred and fifty thousand dollars in compensation for the Everests' having conspired to blow up the Buffalo Oil Company works, entice away its employees, harass it with unfounded law suits, and, somewhat anticlimactically, insult its products. This time Matthews included Archbold, Rogers, and McGregor as defendents in his suit. Then, against the advice of his lawyers, he also sought an indictment for criminal conspiracy to sabotage his plant against the Everests and the three officers of the Standard Oil Company. When the indictment was denied, Matthews tried again; and this time the indictment succeeded.

Now the entire nation took notice of the case. Standard countered with an accusation against Matthews of blackmail in offering his firm for sale to the company. In the process of gathering evidence, Standard agents did not hesitate to pump whiskey into Albert Miller while simultaneously pumping information out. Because Albert reveled in the whiskey, he doubtless revealed much of interest. For, as H. D. Lloyd had sympathetically noted in *Wealth Against Commonwealth*, "Albert was a man infirm under temptation." Miller, weary of a life whose conditions were set by the Everests—making him "a cheap American Faust, revelling in a pinchbeck paradise," added Lloyd—had returned to honest labor in a Pennsylvania refinery. "With all Albert's faults," Lloyd wrote, "he kept one dignity to the end which makes him tower over his seducers—the dignity of labor."[7]

The indictment against Rogers, Archbold, and McGregor was once more quashed for lack of evidence of criminal intent. The Everests were, however, convicted of criminal conspiracy. Sentence was stayed until May, 1888; they were then fined two hundred and fifty dollars each. Matthews had failed financially before the end of the trial, so the court ordered the receiver for his company to accept eighty-five-thousand-dollar damages awarded in his second civil suit against the Everests and to use the sum to settle the company's affairs, paramount among them his lawyers' fees.[8]

Tarbell concluded her account of the unsavory case as cautiously as she began it:

> The case is of importance not only as showing to what abuses the Standard policy of making it hard for a rival to do business will lead men like the Everests, but it shows to what lengths a hostile public will go in interpreting the acts of men who it has come to believe are lawless and relentless in pursuing their ends. The public, particularly the oil public, has always been willing to believe the worst of the Standard Oil Company. It read into the Buffalo case deliberate arson, and charged not only the Everests, but three co-directors, with overt acts. They refuse to recognize that no evidence of the connection of Mr. Rogers, Mr. Archbold and Mr. McGregor with the overt act was offered, but demanded that they be convicted on presumption, and when the judge refused to do this they cursed him as a traitor.[9]

To this statement she added, "no refinery was burned in Buffalo."[10]

In a recent edition of Lloyd's *Wealth Against Commonwealth,* Thomas C. Cochran omitted the original's four chapters devoted to the Buffalo case. Cochran judged Albert Miller's testimony unreliable, and his testimony had been vital in the criminal conspiracy suit of Matthews against the Everests. Sober reflection would lead more readers to agree with Cochran's judgment. Lloyd was a superb journalist, but seems to have possessed the temperament of a novelist. He was carried away by the dramatic possibilities offered by the Buffalo affair, though as a lawyer he was undoubtedly familiar with the unlovely human traits which surface in disputes, and particularly in those over money. Perhaps it was the fanciful Faustian tag he affixed to Miller which misled him. But Albert Miller, his "cheap American Faust," was not so dignified by labor as to conceal from any reasonably observant reader that he appears to have been a two-faced liar willing to do anything for money, as well as a soggy drunkard. Thus the credibility of his evidence seems shaky to a historian like Cochran, no matter how true it may have appeared to a humanitarian like Lloyd.

The case is not germane to Montague's monograph on the Standard Oil Company, and he does not include it. In his later critique of Tarbell's history of the company, however, he accuses her of using in her account of it an emotive language that was calculated to arouse readers' antagonism toward Standard and simultaneously obscure her "genuine conviction that the charge is unfounded."[11] He cannot escape her conclusion, however, that the public was willing to believe the worst of Standard Oil. In frustration he pettishly remarks, "Truly an inadvertent statement of fact which might shock the belief of 'a hostile public' has been successfully avoided in Miss Tarbell's narrative."[12]

Only careless reading or willful wish-fulfillment could lead to the belief that her account involved Standard in the Buffalo imbroglio, but she and Nevins do agree about the Everests' guilt. Nevins concedes that Standard Oil marketing practices that were designed to eliminate competitors included "frequent price-cutting, espionage, dictation to dealers, and other rough tactics." But a fair-minded reader must agree with his belief that sabotage "would have been abhorrent to the Standard leaders."[13]

Yet the possibility of the Standard leaders' direct encouragement of sabotage was not really Tarbell's point: her aim was to demonstrate that they were ultimately responsible for unleashing violently destructive forces employed by extremist subordinates because of the routine use of marketing tactics such as those cited by Allan Nevins. The evidence in the Buffalo case may be, as Nevins claims, "murky and conflicting"; but Tarbell's accusation of moral responsibility is nonetheless clear and unmistakable. If such a view makes

a modern reader comfortably adjusted to the business mores
of the late twentieth century uncomfortable, that does not
necessarily indicate Tarbell was either naïve or was wrong;
it might even prove she was right.

III *Standard Oil and Politics*

There had long been speculation about Standard Oil's
influence over politicians at every level of government, but
such charges were easier to believe than substantiate.
However, the election of H. B. Payne of Ohio to the United
States Senate in 1884 buttressed widely held convictions that
Standard Oil had Ohio politicians firmly in hand, for Payne
was the father of Oliver H. Payne, the treasurer of the company.
The Paynes were a distinguished Cleveland family, and the
senior Payne had been a Democratic representative in Congress for many years. At the age of seventy-four, he aspired
to the Senate in 1883; but his name was not among those
considered by the Democrats of the Ohio legislature that fall.
When his son generated a Payne boom, rumors arose that ample
bribe money was available to legislators at Payne headquarters.
When Payne unexpectedly gained the nomination, the Ohio
press, followed by Eastern newspapers, immediately condemned his selection as fixed. Payne was nonetheless elected.
In 1886, a Republican-controlled Ohio state legislature ordered
an investigation of Payne's election during which over fifty-five
witnesses testified. Their testimony did not prove charges of
bribery, but the state legislature considered the testimony
important enough to send it to the United States Senate for
study. In July, 1886, the Senate Committee on Elections
refused to consider it.

Public clamor arose as Payne's voting record became known.
In 1887, he voted against the Interstate Commerce Bill, and
was called a vassal of the Standard Oil Company. Payne denied
the charge; Standard maintained its customary silence in the
face of criticism from the public. In his defense the Senator
reminded his critics that Standard Oil was Republican in its
politics. In addition, he stated that he owned no Standard
stock, although his admiration for the company was considerable. He declared that "the Standard Oil Company is
a very remarkable and wonderful institution. It has accomplished within the last twenty years of commercial enterprise

what no other company or association of modern times has accomplished."[14] It seems reasonable to an objective analyst to suppose that Senator Payne's admiration for Standard would be reflected in his voting record. But Standard's adamant silence concerning its relations with Payne seemed to many a confession of guilt, and much of the general public became convinced that the company was "using the legislative bodies of the country in its own interests."[15]

Once more the pattern of response of the four writers about Standard Oil is consistent. Lloyd, who loads his evidence, cites Payne's pro-Standard voting record from the time he entered Congress. Tarbell, who puts the onus of accusation on the public and the press, avoids any direct accusation of Payne or Standard Oil. In Montague's attack on her, he is forced to refer to a series of Tarbell's articles which appeared in the New York*American* in February, 1905, entitled "Crimes of the Standard Oil Trust." According to Montague, the articles were inevitably distorted because the *American* was a "sensational newspaper."[16] He admitted that Tarbell had acknowledged in *The History of the Standard Oil Company* that no bribery was ever proven, but he complained that her account made it seem as if there must have been some. Nevins deduces that public acceptance of the truth of the bribery charges against the Paynes and the oil company was a result of a growing antimonopoly movement that arose from the fear that the trusts were becoming too strong for the government to control.[17]

All four writers agree on the undesirability of unchecked monopoly. Montague's solution followed that of classical economics, for in his view "the ever-present possibility" of competition was sufficient to check the power of the Standard Oil Company.[18] Lloyd advocated Christian Socialism as the cure. Tarbell's answer was government regulation of transportation as a first step in legal control, accompanied by a return to the prewar "American Ideal" similar to that extolled by her employer S. S. McClure. Nevins, who wrote his study of Rockefeller and the Standard Oil Company in the 1940's and revised it in the 1950's, had the benefit of hindsight in advocating government regulation to control monopoly. To him, "pure competition" in the Ricardian sense was an "anachronism" following the Civil War; therefore as a "regulatory force in the petroleum industry [it] was quite unworkable."[19] By the time of Franklin D. Roosevelt, Nevins wrote, "the American people had learned much. They looked more tolerantly upon Rockefeller's objective of a completely controlled and efficiently integrated industry. What they chiefly condemned, in retrospect, was not the aim, but the unfair and unsocial practices which had accompanied the achievement and maintenance of that aim."[20]

Ida Tarbell could easily have agreed with Nevins's statement. While she has often been interpreted as being against big corporations on principle, this is not strictly true. She praised, for example, the incorporation in New Jersey of the Oil Regions' own Pure Oil Company, of which her brother William was an officer. Her later laudatory biographies of Elbert H. Gary and Owen D. Young, previously noted, are additional evidence, as is her book *New Ideals in Business*, which appeared in 1916 and anticipated the tone of her later biographies of the two business leaders. All of these testify to her acceptance of big business, as does her enthusiastic support of the early and controversial "scientific management" principles of Frederick W. Taylor, the pioneer efficiency expert. So long as competition remained she had no fear of bigness.

Narrowing the comparison to the two writers, there remains an irreconcilable difference between Tarbell and Nevins. Nevins appears to be a pragmatist and moral relativist in his approach to history. The controlling value in his exhaustive study of Rockefeller and the Standard Oil Company seems to be material progress. An implicit assumption appears to be that if progress continues, necessary corrections of the system promoting it will evolve from the operations of the system automatically, through some mysterious consensus. To Tarbell, on the contrary, values do not emerge from an existential situation, however they may be modified by it; they are prior to and independent of it. Such values are, in her view, as inseparable from business as from all other human endeavor. The long struggle between the Standard Oil Company, the archetypal trust, and its rivals, the independents of the Oil Regions—not to mention millions of consumers—she viewed as "the struggle . . . between Commercial Machiavellianism and the Christian code."[21] Nothing could be more explicit than this judgment.

Yet Tarbell's and Nevins's studies of Rockefeller and the Standard Oil Company are not mutually exclusive. Nor does the latter's supersede Tarbell's because of newer, richer sources, or the sophistication of its historiography. Indeed, Tarbell's history is still very much alive in a recent (1966) Harper Torchbook paperback edition, edited by David M. Chalmers. Rather, the two authors' works are complementary, for the divergence in interpretation between them is philosophical and is logically irreconcilable. A reader must, therefore, examine both in order to arrive at his own interpretation of the history of all modern business, built as it is upon the revolutionary history of the Rockefeller organization. Surely such reading is relevant in this day of conglomerate mergers whose complexities are staggering and whose power to alter society, not for the better, or even the worse, but only for profit, calls for a moral review. The doctrine of historical inevitability as justification for the business juggernaut has proven insufficient. One need not necessarily accept as beyond alteration what merely happens to emerge from the flux. Historians can be prescriptive as well as descriptive; it is time to entertain that proposition, not dismiss it as a means of masking special pleading or outright falsification. So-called descriptive history shares guilt enough for that.

IV *"The Most Famous Woman Journalist in the World"*[22]

After four exhausting years devoted to *The History of the Standard Oil Company*, Tarbell was weary of the subject; but, since the issue remained, she wrote four more articles. These, it turned out, were her last significant contribution to *McClure's*. The first two, which appeared in July and August, 1905, presented a cruelly unflattering character study of John D. Rockefeller; and each was preceded by one of the portraits already mentioned in connection with *The History of the Standard Oil Company* of a ravaged, ruthless man.

Tarbell, a deft hand with a damaging epigraph, chose for these pieces quotations from Machiavelli's *The Prince*. The first read:

A prince should earnestly endeavor to gain the reputation of kindness, clemency, piety, justice, and fidelity to his engagements. He ought to possess these good qualities, BUT STILL retain *such power over*

himself as to display their opposite whenever it may be expedient. . . .
He should make it a rule, above all things, never to utter anything
which does not breathe of kindness, justice, good faith, and piety;
this last quality it is most important to appear to possess as men
in general judge more from appearances than reality. All men have
eyes, but few have the gift of penetration. Everyone sees your exterior,
but few can discern what you have in your heart.[23]

Her text announced, Tarbell proceeded to illustrate it. She
discerned nothing but blackness in Rockefeller's heart from
the time of the abortive South Improvement Company scheme
of 1872 to other secret arrangements with railroads for rebates.
Whatever his thoughts might have been, Tarbell wrote, "it
is certain that Mr. Rockefeller's conscience and courage with-
stood both public disapproval and public education, and that
the principle of getting rich by the use of privileges contrary
to the public good and to the spirit of the laws became a
cardinal one with him from that date."[24]

Thomas Paine had written *The Age of Reason* to rescue
the French people, he said, from atheistic materialism. Paine
was too close to the topic to remain reasonable, and he allowed
himself excesses in his denunciation of Christianity which,
to say the least, defeated his announced purpose. Tarbell fell
into a similar trap: she shared with the people of her native
region a deep hatred of Rockefeller, and it activated her study
of him in these two articles. "Canonize 'business success,'
and men who make a success like that of the Stanard Oil Company become national heroes!" she had warned in *The History
of the Standard Oil Company*.[25] Convinced that Rockefeller
was of the species most despised on the frontier of her youth,
a hypocrite of a peculiarly offensive kind, who taught the Bible
version of the Golden Rule to his Sunday school classes and
practiced the version of it allegedly taught him by his father,
she set out to demolish the whited sepulcher. She left it in
ruins.

In retrospect, these articles are "hatchet jobs" that could
well serve to illustrate the trend toward sensationalism to
which Tarbell herself attributed the decline of muckraking.[26]
Granting her end, to point out to a suggestible public that
money and success are not automatically admirable, one finds
the means she used as questionable in journalism as were
those she accused the Standard Oil Company of using in
business.

The articles on Rockefeller were followed by two on the oil situation in Kansas, but these were merely a replay in another locale of the action of her world-famous book. Scarcely had *The History of the Standard Oil Company* been published when oil discoveries in the Southwestern United States dwarfed those of the Oil Regions. However, the course of their development had paralleled that in Pennsylvania. Independent oil men had done the exploration and taken the risks, and their success had prompted Standard Oil to move into the area and begin a relentless take-over. But Kansas resisted. The Kansas legislature approved a state-owned refinery and passed stiff laws regulating transportation of oil by rail and pipelines. The state refinery was later found unconstitutional by the courts, but the transportation laws remained in force. Disunity, helped along by wastefulness and inefficiency, had led to the downfall of the Pennsylvania independents. Tarbell gave the Kansas oil men good advice rather than the rousing attack on Standard Oil they wanted and expected: "You must make yourselves as good refiners, as good transporters, as good marketers, as ingenious, as informed, as imaginative in your legitimate undertakings as they are in both their legitimate and illegitimate."[27] With the cool candor of a professional publicist, she justified her advice which, predictably, had not been appreciated: "They had got all they could by raising hell, and now they must settle down to doing business."[28]

She never modified her view of the prewar Standard Oil Company. It remained consistent in *The Nationalizing of Business, 1878–1898*, published in 1936 as volume nine in the *History of American Life* series edited by Arthur M. Schlesinger and Dixon Ryan Fox. Nor had she softened appreciably when she commented in 1939 on the company and its founder in her autobiography. In the sole work for which she is now remembered, *The History of the Standard Oil Company*, the author, her subject, and the times had met to produce a masterpiece which has not declined into a period piece. The questioning of American values in the realm of business that she helped initiate not only has continued but has become acute in the 1970's, when industry threatens to make man's very environment unlivable. Perhaps her solution was simplistic; for she never accepted Socialism as the answer, as, for example, Lloyd, Sinclair, and Steffens had. Hers was more "simpleminded," for she saw "not capitalism but an open disregard of decent ethical business practices by capitalists" as the cause of the malaise in American life.[29] And no one has yet disproven her.

In 1905, Ida Tarbell became an international celebrity; at forty-eight, she reached the climax of her career; and the long remainder was one of gradual decline. The gracious accolade of a contemporary of Tarbell's, Charles D. Hazen, then professor of modern history at Columbia University, serves to mark not only the greatness of *The History of the Standard Oil Company* but also the chronological boundary of her enduring achievement. "Miss Tarbell," he said, "is the only historian I have ever heard of whose findings were corroborated by the Supreme Court of the United States."[30]

CHAPTER 6

The American Years

THE year 1905 cancelled out Ida Tarbell's professional triumph with a numbing personal loss, the death of her father. Like many highly gifted nineteenth-century spinsters who were suspended between the old and new orders, Tarbell was deeply attached to her father and had suffered helpless tortures as he lay dying of gastric cancer. The dedication of her Lincoln biography to him had been no empty filial gesture; for, if Lincoln had been to her "the touchstone" of democracy, her father had likewise been a representative democractic man, the perfect expression of the ideal American. He had been a frontiersman who was able to move forward with the times and yet retain the virtues of his heritage—notably, a regard for the rights of others and a sturdy independence. The delicate balance between old times and new achieved by him and other men of the Oil Regions had been callously upset in her estimation, not by inevitable historical forces, but by the ill-directed predatory impulses of one man, John D. Rockefeller. If it is justifiable to suppose that the moral outrage which lends vitality to *The History of the Standard Oil Company* was a very personal one because her father's business had suffered, it seems no coincidence that Franklin Tarbell's death in early spring was shortly followed by his daughter's uncharacteristically vitriolic "character study" of Rockefeller.

Tarbell's insistence on independence seems reason enough for her avoidance of marriage; in addition, her ineradicable aloofness probably caused hints at a distaste for connubial domesticity such as appeared in a much reprinted article written for *The American Magazine* about Chicago's Domestic Relations Court, a new approach toward dealing with social problems. In the article she thus characterized matrimony: "There are in the city of Chicago, let us say, five hundred thousand pairs of men and women who have undertaken to spend their lives in the appalling intimacy of marriage—to create homes where they may rear children."[1] Nevertheless,

93

her independence was severely tested by her father's death; and she was forced as a result to search within herself for strength to surmount the blow. Previously her work had provided a sufficient *raison d'être,* but she now found herself scribbling in a journal in an unusual and uncongenial effort at introspection. "There has come a point when it is life or death-in-life and I am not willing to give up life," she wrote two months after her father's funeral. "If the innermost recesses are to be entered I must go there alone. I am conscious so much of myself is evading me, and this poor little book is a feeble prop in my effort to reach land I've never explored."[2]

A more substantial prop materialized at this crucial juncture in the person of Henry James. No doubt James would have been astonished had he known Tarbell had momentarily appropriated him as a father figure, but such seems to have been the case. She chanced to meet him at a dinner party given by her friends Charles Hazen and his wife. Used to encountering literary types, she doubtless expected James to spend the evening admiring James, but to her delight he did not; instead, he showed genuine interest and concern for her and the other guests. She never saw him again, but he evidently provided the reassurance she needed, for journal entries became sparser after that.[3] The enduring importance to Tarbell of the meeting is demonstrated by an anecdote included in her autobiography. " 'Cherish your contempts,' Henry James advised me once when he had drawn from me a confession of the conflict between my natural dislike of saying anything unpleasant about anybody and the necessity of being cruel, even brutal, if the work I had undertaken was to be truthful in fact and logic. 'Cherish your contempts,' said Mr. James, 'and strength to your elbow.' "[4]

Another important change in Tarbell's life-style occurred at this time. The family home in Titusville had provided roots for her. With her father's passing, these were damaged; and, to restore them, she bought a place of her own near Hartford in the Connecticut countryside. Here she became the family mainstay her father had once been. She presided over a busy household including her mother; the friend of her life, her sister Sarah; and various young relatives. The country place provided the rural and familial ties she sought, and she spent a large part of her time there for the rest of her life when not traveling on assignments or busy in New York. Her roots in middle-class life provided the sap of her outlook, for she had not modified her deep rapport with the Old American stock from which she sprang. Her Connecticut neighbors were not the sophisticated exurbanites already beginning to buy homes in Connecticut but Yankee dirt farmers who looked her over very cautiously. One of them remarked some years later, "Why when she first came here we were scary about having so smart a person for a neighbor, but she ain't that way at all, she's just the same as us folks."[5]

If Tarbell had remained rootless, the continuity of outlook which marks her work could not in all probability have been maintained. For she was a leading defender of the threatened middle America of her day. As such, she articulated the fears and endeavored to shape the objectives of the heretofore dominant white, Anglo-Saxon, Protestant group of which she was inseparably a part and for which she was unceasingly a partisan. In her work, she created a world in its image because she never seriously questioned the values of that world. This world view was her strength and weakness as a writer. All she wrote conveys the sense of justice, the striving for election, and the inherent moral arrogance that the Puritans bequeathed to their descendants. Because she was intelligent and sensitive, however, she rarely allowed righteousness to degenerate into smugness. If she was not as a writer exactly a publican, neither, by a long shot, was she a Pharisee. If she held to the delusion that a few laws and some Supreme Court decisions could turn back the tide and restore the Old America, there seemed sufficient grounds for it. The onset of World War I, which ended such dreams, was almost a decade distant.

I *From* McClure's *to* The American Magazine

Tarbell's journal, which contains sporadic entries, ends with those in 1906 concerned with the breakup of the *McClure's Magazine* staff, which had revolutionized the mass media. This blow was also personally painful, for the spirit which united McClure and his associates had been one of the excitement of discovery and the lure of high adventure. Perhaps because McClure was not only an editorial genius, but also Irish, the gloss of romance suffused his enterprise, providing a style and a warmth that somehow transcended the hardheaded com-

mercial methods which had brought success. Being endowed
with irrepressible creativity, McClure had always been erratic.
Both Tarbell and John Phillips had formerly managed to
temper his wilder impulses, but by 1906 even they could no
longer handle him. Tarbell confided in her journal that she
could not continue at McClure's without Phillips as a buffer
between McClure and his staff, and that possibility was ended,
since the rupture was irreparable. Yet it had been McClure's
uncanny prescience which had brought her fame, and with
it her happiest years, as a part of the magazine. The trouble
between McClure and the members of his organization who
had been with him from the start involved, however, principles
over which they felt there could be no compromise.

The central issue was a scheme that McClure had to construct
a publishing empire which seemed to them a replica of those
they had been condemning for so many years. Indeed, Tarbell's
last article for the magazine could have been directed at
McClure as well as at Rockefeller. The article, entitled
"Commercial Machiavellianism," characterized industrialists
as highly imaginative "poets" with visions of plenty for all—
visions corrupted by greed for money and power.[6] Although
McClure's associates apparently felt that his vision was more
poetic than corrupt, they sensed its dangers for both their image
and that of the magazine. Tarbell, who rejected the project
outright, emphasized its harebrained aspects:

It was in 1906 that Mr. McClure brought home from one of his foraging
expeditions the plan which was eventually to wreck his enterprises. . . . Without consultation with his partners he had organized
a new company, the charter of which provided not only for a McClure's
Universal Journal, but a McClure's Bank, a McClure's Life Insurance
Company, a McClure's School Book Publishing Company, and later
a McClure's Ideal Settlement in which people could have cheap
homes on their own terms. It undertook to combine with a cheap
magazine . . . an attempt to solve some of the great abuses of the
day, abuses at which we had been hammering in McClure's Magazine.
He proposes to do this by giving the trusts a competition which
would draw their teeth.[7]

At first McClure agreed to sell out his interest in McClure's
Magazine to his rebellious partners, but he soon decided he
could not live without it. The upshot was that they sold their

interest to him and bought *The American Magazine,* owned by Frederick L. Colver and edited by Ellery Sedgwick. John S. Phillips, Ray Stannard Baker, Lincoln Steffens, Ida Tarbell, John M. Siddall, Albert Boyden (all of *McClure's* editorial staff), and David A. McKinlay and John Trainor of the business staff, incorporated as the Phillips Publishing Company and assumed control of *The American Magazine.* Ellery Sedgwick then moved to *McClure's,* on the way to his final destination as owner-editor of *The Atlantic Monthly;* and Finley Peter Dunne and William A. White soon left *McClure's* to join the *American Magazine* staff. The new magazine bore from the start a marked resemblance to its parent publication, but it lacked its liveliness.[8]

II   The Tariff in Our Times

Tarbell's years with *The American* were a continuation of her previous career. She had won fame as a historian of business, and her first series for the new magazine was a history of the protective tariff from its inception during the Civil War to the notorious Payne-Aldrich Tariff Act of 1909 which made a mockery of Republican promises of tariff reform. The first series of articles began in December, 1906, and ran through June, 1907; the second resumed in November, 1909, and continued, with some intermissions, until the final article appeared in June, 1911. Thus, a large portion of her time during these years was devoted to study and explication of the intricacies of the tariff policies of the United States. *The Tariff in Our Times,* one of Tarbell's major works, was published in book form by Macmillan in 1911 and was reprinted the following year. The subject was suited to her ability to write clear and interesting analyses of forbidding economic topics. Her analysis emphasized the intimate connection between protective tariffs and the concurrent rise of big business and its political servitor, the Republican party; and she admirably reflected the attitudes of most of her readers about all three.

In the 1880's, when Tarbell was on the staff of *The Chautauquan,* she had concluded that there were in the United States three basic social wrongs, "all curable," she wryly recollected toward the end of her life. These wrongs produced economic depressions and maldistribution of wealth: "discrimination in transportation; tariffs save for revenue only;

private ownership of natural resources."⁹ *The History of the Standard Oil Company* attacked the first wrong, and *The Tariff in Our Times* exposed the protective tariff for what she believed it was—a shell game for the benefit of the real powers behind the government, the trusts. Possibly because of wariness of its ideological implications, she never explored the third wrong—private ownership of natural resourses—that she had so confidently named early in her career.

The subject of the tariff held wide public interest. Tarbell's first series was designed to remove equally wide ignorance. Since she was by no means a tariff expert, she sought advice from Grover Cleveland, with whose politics and tariff policies she agreed. She had come to know him while she was still with *McClure's* when it had been trying to induce Cleveland to write his reminiscences, for which she had been designated "editorial advisor," as she had been for those of Carl Schurz and Charles A. Dana. Although no agreement was reached, she and Cleveland established a friendly working relationship.

The main resource for the early series was library research, however. Consequently, Tarbell herself condemned it as lifeless. For a reader, though, it remains lively and interesting. Willa Cather, who had stayed on as an editor of *McClure's*, reported that she followed the series with an interest she never expected to find for such a topic. For, with Tarbell's ability to focus dramatically on dominant personalities involved in a particular situation, she kept the series moving from peak to peak of action throughout the Great Barbecue and into the early twentieth century. Her thesis was that protective tariffs fostered the interests of the trusts while sacrificing those of workers and consumers under the guise of protecting them, and her indictment is persuasive. Cleveland, who appears as the would-be savior of the common man, is frustrated in his efforts toward tariff reform by the political and business forces aligned against him.

At this point, the tariff series was interrupted; and Tarbell reported in three articles the events leading to the case against the Standard Oil monopoly conducted in 1907 by the federal government. The series was entitled "Roosevelt vs. Rockefeller"; the title conveys the dragon-slayer role assigned to Roosevelt. The articles are shriller in tone than *The History of the Standard Oil Company*, and they are an updating of

her 1905 account for *McClure's* of Standard's depredations
in Kansas. They served to remind the public that Standard's
ways had not changed. Another short series about the effects
of reform politics in Chicago followed before the tariff series
was resumed.

The new series concentrated on tariff abuses against consumers and workers caused by the cynical manipulations of
lobbyists who represented business interests and con-
gressmen, who also represented them. Tarbell attacked the
resultant harm to families whose average income was three-
hundred fifty dollars a year; to thirteen million other, more
prosperous families whose income was under two thousand
dollars, the average being around five hundred dollars; and
to single working women whose weekly wage was six to
eight dollars. With wrathful irony she posed a somewhat
rhetorical question:

Admitting if you will that it *was* just to make the people of this
country, on $2 a day and less, pay the major share of the cost of
the Civil War, the cost of reconstruction, the cost of establishing
all sorts of industries and protecting them through long terms of years
from the competition of the world, has the time not come when the
Committee on Way and Means can be asked ... to ease the burden
which the protective tariff places today on millions of American
families—tens of thousands of lonely working women living on
incomes where every penny counts?[10]

Since Congress' answer to the query was the outrageous
Payne-Aldrich Act that boosted tariffs to yet new heights, the
relevance of the question is clear, as is that of the series as
a whole. The series was of great importance in informing a
helpless public about how it was being exploited before reform
could be effective. The wrongs committed by Standard Oil
had generally been public knowledge, but tariff manipulation
was done in the dark.

Tarbell turned next on Rhode Island Senator Nelson W.
Aldrich, a foremost architect of protection. "Mr. Aldrich's
'Protection,'" she accused, "is hand in glove with every other
Privilege—naturally it is for the same tribe. It is the friend
and abettor of railroad tyranny, of corporate violence, of
monopoly and manipulation. It is the friend of Wall Street,
the enemy of Conservation, the hope of oligarchy, and the

opponent of property and opportunity" for the average man.[11] As in *The History of the Standard Oil Company,* she uncompromisingly stated that "simmered down to its final sense the tariff question as it stands in this country today is a question of national morals."[12]

Again, the basis for morality was individualism and the general welfare. Are average citizens "better or worse ... less greedy, more spiritual, more self-reliant" as a result of a given institution? This was the standard of judgment, for "principle must in the end control, and one cannot in the end separate morals and economics, for all that people do is moral in the sense that the welfare of society as a whole depends on action."[13] Thus, *The Tariff in Our Times* is a corollary of Tarbell's other, greater muckraking achievement; and together these two books represent her main contribution to the muckraking movement. The secularized morality they defended is the same as that underlying all attacks then and now on the increasingly debatable status of the American Dream which, most still believe, sparked the Declaration of Independence.

III *Ida Tarbell and Feminism*

Feminism was an even livelier topic than today in the years preceding World War I. Ida Tarbell's stand again reveals her conservatism—her innate impulse to create the new order by extending rather than eliminating the old one. She remained immovably convinced that the hand that rocked the cradle ruled enough of the world and did not need to mark a ballot. As it is today, the feminist movement then was allied with other leftist causes vigorously combating the plutocracy which seemed about to take over the country. Tarbell set to work, when she was again removed from the tariff project, researching and writing a history of the feminist movement in the United States.

The result was a series of seven articles which ran from November, 1909, to May, 1910. Entitled *The American Woman,* the series exhibits an antifeminist bias not surprising in a biographer who had decided that Madame Roland would have accomplished more by mending her husband's socks than she had by shaping his politics. In *The American Woman,* which is concise and readable, Tarbell endeavors to demonstrate that women had not truly been overshadowed by men in America but had been coequals with them in developing American civilization, as she herself had observed in the frontier Oil Regions. Abolition and the women's rights movement had been closely connected before the Civil War, but abolition had, however, taken precedence. Following the war, the movement had again become active, reaching its height during the Progressive era under militant feminists impervious to ridicule or to arrest, which they regarded as the symptoms of fear and guilt in American society over the repression of women. Tarbell countered their militancy with the thesis that women's rights, like their place, reside in the home.

She cited Abigail Adams and Mercy Warren as examples of liberated women worthy of emulation. According to Tarbell, they had been content to employ their talents for the American Revolutionary cause without assuming public roles, for they had been indifferent to the legal formality of equal rights so long as they felt they possessed them in fact. As early as the 1780's however, Condorcet, a friend and associate of Madame Roland, began advocating the right for women to vote and hold public office. An aristocrat himself, he recognized that the advantages granted to privileged women like Abigail Adams and Mercy Warren must be legally guaranteed to ordinary women. Tarbell, so insistent on legal equality and equality of opportunity for men, never very seriously considered either for women; for, to her, they were primarily creators and preservers of civilized values. Thus, competition with men for equal rights could divert women from their vital social roles and upset the delicate balance of influence between the sexes in society, and could transform women into counterfeits of men instead of counterparts of them. Essentially, she was reacting against the breakdown of family life which had accompanied industrialism.

Tarbell's research showed that the status of women had been advanced by two wars, the Revolution and the Civil War; for women had enlarged their activities from their homes to their communities. She envisioned women in such roles in the national community, closely bound to their homes, but available for service to the national family. Like most contemporary progressives, she was primarily interested in preserving American social norms; therefore, the individual was secondary, regardless of rhetoric to the contrary. Women were thus to her counters in the game of history rather than individuals entitled to unique fulfillment. With the easy certainty of the childless, Tarbell evidently assumed that other women fulfilled themselves solely through their husbands and children. Her knowledge of feminine psychology was not profound.

Tarbell doubtless expressed the view of the silent majority of her time, however vehemently the vocal minority of feminists rejected her. Possibly that silent majority still exists. Certainly Nancy Reagan, wife of California's Governor Ronald Reagan, apparently believes so. When recently asked her reaction to the current women's liberation movement, she echoed Ida Tarbell: "Part and parcel of being a woman," said the governor's wife, "is to be a mother and homemaker.... It's part of being a man to be a breadwinner and provider for your family. If you mix the two together and make them one you have unhappy people. They cheat themselves out of one of the great experiences of being a woman, I think."[14] While Tarbell could still hope in her day to turn back the tide, no room remains for doubt that American culture has decreed that Mrs. Reagan, however well she understands the art of public relations or how sincere she may be in her statement, has much to learn about economics, that implacable arbiter of domestic mores. What is more, the population explosion has made motherhood unprecedentedly suspect.

Tarbell and D. H. Lawrence share a certain similarity in their views regarding women, unlikely as it may seem. Tarbell constructed a model Mrs. America for a doll-house nation, whereas Lawrence created a mythic earth goddess who offered sex as salvation. But both writers were reacting to the erosion of family life resulting from industrialism, and both believed that women were being exploited and depersonalized—and could prevent it, if they realized what was happening. One might not agree with either, but their concern and their integrity demand respect. Neither writer granted women what more and more of them were coming to demand, the right to be human beings as well as women; for both were doctrinaire theorists who were as stubborn as their opponents, the militant doctrinaire feminists.

Tarbell's views about women struck a resounding chord of popular conservatism which evoked two additional series, both published by Macmillan after being serialized. The first, *The Business of Being Woman,* appeared throughout 1912 in *The American Magazine.* In it, the author, who very ingeniously adapted the scientific management principles of Frederick Taylor to home management, characteristically postulated that modernization of the traditional domestic sphere would promote social stability. The vote for women was to her a peripheral concern; for, as she declared, "the central fact of a woman's life, Nature's reason for her, is the child, his bearing and rearing. There is no escape from the divine order that her life must be built around this constraint, duty, or privilege, as she may please to consider it."[15]

The second series which appeared in the *Ladies' Home Journal* during 1913, was entitled *The Ways of Women;* and it emphasized parallels between twentieth-century women and their predecessors. Although *The Ways of Women* contains much of the tart common sense Tarbell abundantly possessed, the book is superficial; but it is not dishonest. Tarbell managed to implement her readers' egos without unduly insulting their intelligence, a feat expected of writers for women's magazines by editors with a budget suspended over their heads like the sword of Damocles. The intelligent, aristocratic Ideal Woman—a sort of eternalized Abigail Adams—was portrayed as a model of emulation for the housewives of the rising working class.

Even *The American's* editor John Phillips, whose views generally coincided with Tarbell's, chided her for her refusal to espouse woman's suffrage. Stung, she defended herself in a letter to him which, to be fair, should be extensively quoted:

You want me to explain my position on the extension of suffrage to women. You declare that it seems to you illiberal and contradictory—that it disappoints your idea of my mind and character. You have intimated that I am kept out of the present movement by vanity—that is—having several years ago allowed the use of my name in a protest against the extension of suffrage to women at that time, that I am too proud to admit I might have been wrong—which is to say I have not the "self-correcting conscience." You also seem to be coming to the conclusion that what Helen Keller is reported to have said of me not long ago is true—that is, that I am getting too old to understand and sympathize with the aspirations of a growing world!

It is quite probable that there is at least a suspicion of truth in all that you say. I have always found it difficult to explain myself, even to myself, and I do not often try. However, the fact that I am one of your staff on *The American Magazine,* as well as one of your regular contributors, the fact that I know how deeply you have it at heart that the magazine should in its own way encourage free experimenting with life makes me feel rather in duty bound to try to put down as honestly as I can what I do think in the matter.... There is in feminine nature a strange barrier against complete self-revelation.... You see my feeling about suffrage is different from that of a great number of people of today because I was really born to the idea, and considerable [numbers] of both the men and the women active in the movement now seem to have heard, or at least thought of it, for the first time.

I grew up among people who believed in women's suffrage as much as they did in the abolition of slavery, the observance of the Sabbath, or the beneficence of the protective tariff. It was part of the creed I learned as a child—a part of the liberal program of the day. Elizabeth Cady Stanton and Susan B. Anthony were grouped in my young girl's mind with William Lloyd Garrison and General Grant and Abraham Lincoln and Geo. M. Curtis and Horace Greeley and Carl Schurz. I took suffrage as one of the great "rights" that women were born into the world for the express purpose of acquiring... a college education was another... to go to a man's college and fit myself for a man's work—that was to be my contribution to the cause![16]

At college, she became disenchanted with women's suffrage, perhaps partly because she found much to admire in the masculine world she invaded there and ever afterwards preferred. Her own attitude toward women is pretty well summed up in an Englishwoman's remark she included in her letter to Phillips: "The only reason I am glad that I am a woman is that I will not have to marry one." No remark could better attest to Tarbell's utter femininity.

In summary, Tarbell's view about women that she had articulated in *Madame Roland* provided the basis for all her writing on women. She wanted to conserve and channel the immense moral force she imputed to them, and she felt that suffrage would tend to dissipate it. She assured Phillips that she was not hostile to women's suffrage, but merely indifferent, since the vision of a better life for all had been sighted without it. "This look into the possibilities of life for all," she earnestly continued,

has been accompanied—is perhaps explained by a spreading conviction that the things which have so largely defeated life for the many
are unnecessary. Poverty is not necessary; war which is the chief
cause of poverty is not necessary. They are the ogres which have
shut off happy, full lives from the great mass of the earth and they
must go. Women, like men, are after them. They would legislate
them out of the world—and they rush for the tools with which to
make the attack. But it can't be done that way. Poverty and war
and privilege are the children of greed and selfishness and unbridled
natures. *Nothing but the slow processes of education will put an
end to them* [italics added], and believing this how can I fight for
that [suffrage] which I believe will hamper the direct use of the
tools which will do the work.

You will gather from this that the chief reason I am not interested
in the extension of suffrage is because I feel that it is part of what
seems to me the most dangerous fallacy of our times—and that is
that we can be saved morally, economically, socially by laws and
systems.[17]

Tarbell's flat rejection of revolutionary changes like those
advocated by Madame Roland or effected by John D. Rockefeller shaped her response. She needed the assurance of the
continuity of evolutionary change; but, in the case of feminism,
her gradualism turned reactionary. While the problems of black
people, about which her colleague Ray Stannard Baker was
writing, did not seem to concern her, she surely would not
have advocated repeal of the Fifteenth Amendment that
guaranteed black men suffrage. And the Twenty-first Amendment, ratified after World War I, was the logical culmination
of over one hundred years of agitation for women's suffrage.
No, Tarbell's upside-down utopianism blinded her to the
exploitation of women that laws could and did rectify. She
had written in favor of the ten-hour day for women because
it would make them better housewives and mothers than those
thousands who worked even longer hours could possibly
become. Yet she did not wish to grant women a direct role
in realizing their goals. This attitude seems certainly an
implicit declaration that she shared the opinion of those who
regarded women as second-rate citizens, and possibly that her
view of women's role in society was hopelessly sentimental,
as well as patronizing.

It seems inconsistent for Tarbell to devote the major effort
of her career to helping procure laws regulating American

business and to fight at the same time a law in the interest
of American women, the suffrage amendment. Actually no such
inconsistency is present; government regulation by the laws
of business and by the apron strings of women were both
important parts of her vision, her American Dream. As visions
tend to be, hers was solipsistic. But, like all visions of a better
society, hers was nevertheless a valuable one because it presented options for consideration by the members of her society,
who validate or invalidate visions.

IV *The Golden Rule in Business*

Ida Tarbell's last contribution to *The American Magazine*
formalized her wholehearted acceptance of the new business
order. The series derived from her observations of vicious
labor exploitation while she was gathering data for her series
about the tariff. At that time, she had "taken satisfaction in
presenting the worst conditions . . . badly ventilated and dangerous factories, unsanitary homes, underfed children." At the
same time, she had taken note of "substantial and important
efforts . . . to improve conditions, raise wages, shorten hours,
humanize labor relations" among a significant number of
enlightened owners and managers.[18]

A journalist above all else, Tarbell scented a good story
and correctly sensed the public's mood which, before 1910
or thereabouts, had welcomed exposure of the dark side of
business. Why not now reveal the sunny side? The result was
The Golden Rule in Business, a well-researched series which
ran in *The American* for a year, ending in September, 1915.
Immediately published by Macmillan as *New Ideals in
Business: An Account of Their Practice and Their Effects upon
Men and Profits*, this work was followed in 1920 by a French
version, *La Règle d'Or des Affaires*. Fifty-five firms were
covered in the study as most illustrative of the new trend,
though Tarbell visited many more.

The Golden Rule in Business was a popularization of the
scientific management methods of Frederick W. Taylor at the
tag end of the era which equated science with salvation. Taylor
had begun his experiments in scientific management in 1882
with job analyses of the tasks of laborers in the Philadelphia
plant of the Midvale Steel Company, but his ideas had been
slow to catch on in the United States. By 1911, however, profits

had dropped, the rate of industrial expansion had slowed, and costs consequently needed cutting. Taylor's ideas then gained the hearing in the United States that they had achieved in Europe ten years previously, and he published a book about his methods in 1911. Tarbell's series provided concrete evidence that Taylor's system worked. Her thesis was "Humanity Is the Foundation of Good Business."

The articles dealt with various segments of industry in turn: the rising status of workers, new safety measures, housing improvements for workers, stock sharing and other fringe benefits being offered to them, and the benefits of shorter hours and recreational facilities. Full title of the series was *The Golden Rule in Business: How It Pays in Dollars and Cents, Personal Satisfaction, Human Happiness.* The priorities given the benefits listed reveal the line of argument, for Tarbell was writing in an era that was just recognizing that production is helped rather than hindered by good treatment of workers, an idea theretofore thought of as wildly paradoxical and as completely irrelevant to the business world, if not immoral.

"Death and mutilation," Tarbell postulated, "are no longer considered the will of the Lord."[19] Tarbell defended the Taylor method, which was to her a necessary accompaniment to the achievement of the Golden Rule among workers. To Labor critics who attacked Taylor's methods as a disguised form of exploitation, she furnished a detailed reply. She listed and attempted to rebut the major criticisms of them:

1. The system was a speed-up.

She denied the charge, explaining that since it took six years to complete installation of the Taylor system, many imitations taking a shorter time had sprung up which were indeed no better than speed-ups.

2. Workers are timed as a prod to laggards.

Not so. Workers are timed in order to train them to use more efficient methods.

3. Taylor training lessens the number of workers needed and produces unemployment.

Tarbell replied that, on the contrary, the system produced new jobs; and displaced workers could thus be relocated in the new openings.

4. The system caused overproduction with consequent unemployment.

"Work breeds work," Tarbell countered. A consumer economy
ensures high employment.
  5. The system was antiunion.
Tarbell argued that the system encourages such genuine
cooperation between management and labor that unions would
not need to protect workers from previous abuses.
  6. The system would destroy collective bargaining.
Tarbell admitted that this was a possibility. She thought that
only labor leaders trained under the system could decide,
though she felt it posed no real threat.[20]
Tarbell's book was a powerful agent in humanizing the
attitudes of management and of the general public toward the
plight of workers in industry. Her articles on industrial relations that offered the Golden Rule, combined with efficiency
charts, as a solution to exploitation and other industrial ills
made readers recognize that foreign workers, far from improv-
ing their lives in the United States, had often found themselves
in worse straits than before. Moreover, the articles clearly
demonstrated that better treatment of workers resulted in greater profits for factory owners. The fundamental failure in
industry, Tarbell believed, was dehumanization; and she
dramatized her point by describing a case of industrial murder
which had occurred at the Roosevelt Borough plant of the
Fertilizer Trust, located in Middlesex County, a twenty-
minute ride from the New York City Hall where the United
States Industrial Commission was conducting hearings concerning industrial abuses. Eighteen strikers had been killed
by strikebreakers without provocation. When Tarbell left the
New York hearings to investigate the murders, a radical friend
asked bitterly if she had gone there expecting to find the
Golden Rule. She imperturbably replied that she had gone to
determine whether the Golden Rule could have prevented
the slaughter.
The fertilizer plant's workers were unorganized immigrants
who had finally struck because of intolerable working conditions. Their pay was $1.60 per day; their hours were long;
they had no protection from dangerous machinery and no compensation worthy of the name for injuries. Seasonal layoffs
and a nauseating smell that clung to clothes and bodies were
additional complaints. Tarbell reported that the immigrant
workers were ridiculed and misused by employers who

regarded them as animals; the murder had been akin to slaughtering cattle in the minds of those responsible. If Elbert H. Gary, president of the United States Steel Corporation, could humanize the steel industry, Tarbell asked, why couldn't the operators of the Fertilizer Trust have done the same? Therefore, she concluded in answer to her own question, the Gary Golden Rule could indeed have prevented the slaughter.[21]

Tarbell's concern for the plight of workers was genuine, but the tone of her *Golden Rule in Business* lacks the cutting edge of moral commitment which animates *The History of the Standard Oil Company*. In it Tarbell fought for her own, the native Old Americans of the Oil Regions; but her approach in *The Golden Rule in Business* seems condescending and paternalistic toward the working-class immigrants. Their situation is presented as a problem resolvable by the Taylor method. The cold-cash practicality of *The Golden Rule in Business* unduly stresses that improved working conditions were good for business, and a reader is almost forced to assume that they were also good for the workers themselves.

Nevertheless, Tarbell's point holds. Workers who had been cruelly exploited under the Gospel of Wealth were less so by 1914. In retrospect, Tarbell defended herself against charges of accommodation by saying that

many of my reforming friends were shocked because the only reason most industrial leaders gave for their experiments [with the Taylor method] was that it paid. Certainly they sought dividends; but they believed stability, order, peace, progress, cooperation were back of dividends . . . so in spite of the charge of many of my friends that I was going over to the enemy, joining the corporation lawyer and the company nurse, I clung to the new ideals. What I never could make some of my friends see was that I had no quarrel with corporate business so long as it played fair. . . . I had no quarrel with men of wealth if they could show performance back of it untainted by privilege.[22]

The Golden Rule in Business tacitly announced the end of muckraking as a livelihood and as a movement. When *The American Magazine* was sold in 1915 to the Crowell Publishing Company, the staff which had moved to it from *McClure's* quickly disbanded. The magazine was converted into an unchallenging, "wholesome" periodical for men under the

editorship of John Siddall, whom Tarbell had brought to
McClure's as a young research assistant. At Siddall's insistence,
John Phillips was retained as a consulting editor. Thus, with
the ending of the world that the journal knew, one of the
great Progressive journals faded away; and, although the Muckrakers met the strange world which beset them with the onset
of World War I courageously, most of them never fully understood it. Ida Tarbell, among the most indomitable of them,
began a new career at an old stand: she signed a contract
to deliver a series of Chautauqua lectures based on the ideas
and practices she had propagandized in *The Golden Rule in
Business.*

CHAPTER 7

A New Career in a Changed World

IN an effort to counter alienation among individuals, twentieth-century mass societies elevate certain outstanding individuals to the status of culture heroes. These equivalents of the folk heroes of simpler agrarian cultures answer the same need to provide relief from the drabness of ordinary life or to furnish attractive sanctions for desirable attitudes. Not so durable as great legendary figures like Abraham Lincoln, their vogue represents current rather than timeless values. They may be actors, politicians, athletes, poets, playboys—never plowboys. Robert Frost was a culture hero of the 1950's and 1960's; already, following his death he is being diminished in stature by biographers. Not only had Frost captured in his poetry the essence of a national mood, but he also aged charmingly. He thus became a virile patriarchal figure for many Americans, who found in both his work and his public personality sanity and strength—an individuality Americans desperately needed to affirm in their beehive cities. His "lover's quarrel with the world" was solidly reassuring in an era demanding that liberal dashes of irony lace its affirmation; a statement of faith less tentative than Frost's would have been ridiculed.

Ida Tarbell was such a culture hero, or heroine, between the two world wars. Muckraking crusader for the middle class, liberated New Woman who yet remained womanly, promoter of the values of Old America, and a person of unquestioned integrity, she was a sort of national maiden aunt who was "beautiful with virtue," as Ray Stannard Baker once said of her. She spoke for the majority on the woman question and on big business; she was an inexhaustible source of Lincoln lore. *The History of the Standard Oil Company* was ranked as her greatest achievement, but it was by no means regarded as her only one. Today, she is remembered, if at all, for that book alone. She was fifty-eight in 1915, and her eyes met the world's with calm, good-humored appraisal; like Frost, she aged well; and her gaze in the years to follow remained serene, though not always so without effort.

I Lecturer and War Worker

Lecture tours for the Chautauqua Circuit provided a new medium for Tarbell, theretofore known mainly as a writer. The return brought her back to her beginnings as an editor for The Chautauquan during the 1880's in spirit. But actually she had never strayed far from the earnest, intelligent, socially minded aims of the magazine for which she first worked. In addition to lecturing, she became a free-lance journalist, writing a series for the Woman's Home Companion pleading with women not to jettison their tried and true traditional identity in favor of one untested and, she implied, untrue to women in their proper role as bastions of the family. These articles were published as The Ways of Woman by Macmillan in 1915, for serialization followed by publication was still profitable for popular writers; and, like most writers, Tarbell was thrifty with ideas and careful with contracts, knowing full well that the former were scarce and valuable and that the latter bore watching. After the United States declared war in April, 1917, she became a hard-working member of the national Women's Committee of the Council of National Defense.

The concepts of Frederick Taylor's scientific management methods that she had written about in The Golden Rule in Business formed the basis of her Chautauqua lectures. And they also provided a rationale for The Ways of Woman, for Tarbell was convinced that efficient work methods in homes would work wonders there in addition to making the job of housekeeping more challenging, thereby encouraging women to stay at home. Her appointment to the Women's Committee of the Council of National Defense in the spring of 1917 resulted from her propaganda experience as a Muckraker and her widely read commentaries about women in the modern world. The militant feminists on the committee, including their chairwoman Dr. Anna Shaw, objected at first to Tarbell's inclusion; but they soon found her flexible and easy to work with, despite her disavowal of their aggressive attempts to secure autonomy for women.

When President Wilson had first asked Tarbell, in December, 1916, to become a member of the important Tarriff Commission for which he considered her well qualified, she had rejected him. Even *The Nation,* always cool toward her, managed grudging praise about her qualifications. Where "hundreds of writers" had failed, *The Nation'*s Washington correspondent conceded, she had "come nearer than any other to stripping a technical subject of its redundant technicalities, and reducing it to a point where the intelligent, though unlearned, can grasp it mentally. For she has a well-whetted analytical faculty and a gift for popular interpretation."[1] But the inevitable belittlement appeared as *The Nation'*s correspondent warmed to his work:

> If there is one thing more noticeable than another in Miss Tarbell's manner as a writer, it is her definiteness, whereas her most striking characteristic in personal intercourse is her moderation. Her whole appearance speaks this. Of good height and slender but strong figure, with a face well balanced in features and thoroughly feminine in cast, eyes that are both sincere and pleasant in expression, and a nicely modulated voice, there is not about her the slightest suggestion of "opinionation" as we commonly use the term, yet, though a broad charity forbids her confusing men and things, her views on most public matters are positive to a degree. She has a kindly word for Pig-Iron Kelley [a protective tariff manipulator lengthily discussed in *The Tariff in Our Times*] and his economic kindred, but this does not move her to spare the ruling tariff system on either its material or moral side. It is the old story of loving the sinner but hating the sin. . . .[2]

The writer then declared that Tarbell's position on the tariff was too inflexible for her to become an effective member of the Tariff Commission.

Tarbell's reasons for refusing Wilson's invitation are not only characteristic but demonstrate her integrity and common sense, qualities for which she was held in esteem:

> First, there was my personal situation,—my obligations. I had no right to give up my profession for a connection of that sort, in its nature temporary. Then I realized my own unfitness as Mr. Wilson could not. I had no experience in the kind of work this required. I was an observer and reporter, not a negotiator. . . . But primarily there was my hopelessness about the service the Tariff Commission might render. Its researches and conclusions, however sound, would

stand no chance in Congress when a wool or iron and steel or sugar
lobby appeared. A Tariff Commission was hamstrung from the start.

Jane Addams pleaded with me to accept "for the sake of women,"
but I did not feel women were served merely by an appointment
to office. Women, like men, serve in proportion to their fitness for
office, to the actual fact they have something to contribute. I had
no enthusiasm for the task, did not even respect it greatly.... The
cause of women is not to be advanced by putting them into positions
for which they are untrained.[3]

President Wilson's offer of a place on the Tariff Commission
had followed an interview with him that she had written for
Collier's just before the presidential election in November.
Wilson had evidently been evaluating her views while she
probed his on behalf of a public which had seen little of him
during the campaign. The politician in Wilson unerringly per-
ceived the role she expected of him. He was, she enthusiasti-
cally reported, "as open as a book . . . never have I talked with
any man who showed himself more direct, less engaged with
himself and more engaged with the affairs committed to him,
more just and more gentle in his estimate of people, and yet
never for an instant fooled. Mr. Wilson is a fine, humorous,
cultivated American gentlemen . . . a president, yes, every
instant; but also a gentleman, who, having invited you to his
table, treats you as a fellow human being, interested in the
things he is interested in and frankly willing to talk them
over *with* you, not *at* you."[4]

Wilson's personality dazzled Tarbell, and his conquest of
her was complete when the issues which interested him were,
judging from the contents of the interview, the same as those
dear to her—for the remainder of the interview recounts his
positions on her favorite topics. It is oddly as if Tarbell had
projected through Wilson her deepest beliefs; so perfectly
attuned was she to the ineffable white, Anglo-Saxon, Protestant
consciousness they both shared that she could faultlessly trans-
mit it at its truest pitch when she found the right medium.
Not only was Wilson right; it was almost as though he were
an embodiment of Lincoln. Indeed, he compared his situation
in 1916 with that of Lincoln in the 1864 election.

Wilson professed himself a pragmatist rather than a theoreti-
cian in politics. His first response to a new idea, wrote Tarbell,
was "Will it work?" He then condemned Wall Street efforts

to secure special privileges through control of the banks; for he viewed the election, he assured her, as a contest between "privilege and the people." She was truly impressed also with his genuine knowledge of tariff problems; in addition, Wilson ingratiated himself in her regard when he said he believed in the sanctity of work, favored the eight-hour day, and had a favorable attitude to Taylor's scientific management ideas.

The interview concluded with the exact blend of lofty principle and shrewd practicality which also characterized Ida Tarbell. Wilson explained that he thought that to conduct a campaign during that moment of crisis in national affairs would be in bad taste; then he confided, as one realist to another, "I am inclined to think that bad taste is bad politics."[5] Wilson, who was as skilled as Theodore Roosevelt had been in gaining the loyalty of reporters, had made a permanent supporter of Tarbell. So loyal was she that she continued to support the League of Nations despite its rejection by the Senate and the public, and she continued unwavering in her belief that peace could be attained through international cooperation. She could well have said that in this instance she had remained true to principle while the majority, in whom she had such mystical faith, had succumbed to despair.

In the meantime, she continued lecturing, finding life on the circuit varied and interesting, though she became inclined to rate towns on the quality of their hotel beds. She discovered in her audiences of everyday people a healthy corrective; for, as a writer, she had not had to contend with audiences who could counter her positions. As a speaker, she soon was able to sense disagreement or resistance, even when it was unspoken. And she learned to live with apathy, the bane of all lecturers.

While speaking before working-class audiences about Taylor's scientific management and the "new ideals in business," she realized the insubstantiality of his methods. For one thing, the management point of view they represented had tended to obscure for her the plight of most workers, which she was soon forced to recognize when she spoke near the grubby industrial settlements in which they lived. However much faith she might have in the ultimate efficacy of Taylor's methods, the reality before her indicated otherwise. Her audiences were too polite or too inarticulate to dispute her, but their apathy told the tale.

A subject of prime interest to both lecturer and audience was the war. Like most, Tarbell had been a Pacifist. Just before the war began she had been planning a series of antiwar articles in collaboration with David Starr Jordan, president of Stanford University and a leading Pacifist. Jordan's advocacy of elimination of international trade barriers in the interest of world peace appealed to Tarbell's antitariff bias. She visited the Stanford campus for several weeks, observing peace activists without finding a suitable angle for a story. Finally, she and Jordan decided to write a series to be called "The Case Against War." Then the war broke out, ending the illusion they shared with millions that good will and rationality would eliminate war from the earth. When Tarbell became convinced that the entry of the United States was inevitable, she shed her illusion earlier in the conflict than did other liberals who clung to the hope that the United States could remain neutral.[6]

The entry of the United States in April, 1917, abruptly changed Tarbell's views about serving on government committees; and she immediately accepted her appointment to the Women's Committee, as did the noted feminist Carrie Chapman Catt. Tarbell's war tasks were congenial, for they followed her concept that woman's role is supportive; but the militants on the committee resented its auxiliary role to the all-male Council of Defense. Consequently, Tarbell found herself often acting as mediator between the two committees. She abandoned all her own work plans, aside from the lecture tour she had signed for before April, one that took her on a twenty-five-thousand-mile journey through twenty-five states. She saw war fever mount and, more and more rarely, encountered irreconcilable Pacifists who whispered their defiance, for few had the stubborn courage of Randolph Bourne, who continued to write against United States involvement until all channels were closed to him. Tarbell, with her usual moderation, heard the antiwar advocates out; she defended Pacifists like Jane Addams against the attacks of superpatriots; and she refused Henry Ford's urgent invitation to sail on his Peace Ship. Her inner torment was intense, for her world, a nineteenth-century one, had ended in August, 1914; and she now had to come to terms with a new age. Perhaps in an attempt to put this overwhelming experience into some sort of perspective, she began her only published novel, one which recounted in narrative form the transition of America from provincialism to internationalism during World War I.

II   The Rising of the Tide: The Story of Sabinsport

Henry Adams described an American ambiguity which has always puzzled foreigners: the volatile mixture of genuine idealism and calculating materialism which so often motivates Americans, lending what seems to outsiders a specious elevation to what is actually sordid enterprise. When Adams anatomized this confusing trait in the scruffy frontiersmen of 1800 in his *History of the United States of America during the First Administration of Thomas Jefferson,* he viewed the American, crude in the wilderness or in the tavern, as an "unconscious poet" bathed in "an atmosphere which the self-conscious poet could not penetrate." He termed Abraham Lincoln the representative American because of his effortless admixture of idealism and practicality. Even on the most practical plane, wrote Adams, the American's "hyperbole of enthusiasm" seemed visionary to Europeans who lived in the present; for Americans lived in the future:

"Look at my wealth!" cried the American to his foreign visitor. "See these solid mountains of salt and iron, of lead, copper, silver, and gold! See these magnificent cities scattered broadcast to the Pacific! See my cornfields rustling and waving in the summer breeze from ocean to ocean, so far that the sun itself is not high enough to mark where the distant mountains bound my golden seas! Look at this continent of mine, fairest of created worlds, as she lies turning up to the sun's never-failing caress of her broad and exuberant breasts, overflowing with milk for her hundred million children! See how she glows with youth, health, and love!" Perhaps it was not altogether unnatural that the foreigner, on being asked to see what needed centuries to produce, should have looked about him with bewilderment and indignation. "Gold! cities! cornfields! continents! Nothing of the sort! I see nothing but tremendous wastes, where sickly men and women are dying of home-sickness or are scalped by savages! mountain-ranges a thousand miles long, with no means of getting to them, and nothing in them when you get there! swamps and forests choked with their own rotten ruins! nor hope of better for a thousand years! Your story is a fraud, and you are a liar and a swindler!"

Met in this spirit, the American, half perplexed and half defiant, retaliated by calling his antagonist a fool ... for himself he cared little, but his dream was his whole existence.[7]

Tarbell, whose prose never soared like Adams's, nevertheless wrote from the same understanding. By the time of World
War I, Americans had seen actualized much of the future predicted by Adams's frontiersman and by Thomas Jefferson when
he engineered the Louisiana Purchase; and fulfillment had
come in far less time then the millennia predicted for it by
those true believers. But Americans still universally believed
that there was more, much more, in the American dream. *The
Rising of the Tide* is not a good novel, but Tarbell captures
in it this visionary quality. Implicit also in the novel is a restriction of the dream which neither Adams nor Tarbell made
explicit. The restriction was that the dream had been appropriated by the dominant Anglo-Saxon culture of the United
States which had come to feel that it alone had shaped the
dream and therefore had a right to dictate who should share
it and on what terms.

The experiences of her twenty-five-thousand-mile journey
around the country were distilled by Tarbell into the story
of one small Midwestern town during the years between the
onset of the war in 1914 and the Armistice in 1918. In the
novel the town was called Sabinsport, and was situated on
the Ohio River twenty-five miles from Cincinnati. But it could
have been Titusville, or better yet Poland, Ohio, where she
had taught school for two years after graduation from Allegheny
College. The narrative depicts the shift in attitude among the
fifteen thousand townsmen toward the war and, as a result
of it, toward each other. Beginning with isolationism and
laissez-faire individualism, they gradually develop a sense of
community as the profound worldwide implications of the
struggle are brought home to them through the involvement
of fellow townsmen in the war and through their own war
effort. The town's class divisions are clearly indicated, from
the white, Anglo-Saxon, Protestant aristocracy and middle
class, to the Irish, Slavic, and Southern European servants and
workers who constitute the lower orders.

Ralph Gardner, muckraking young editor of the town newspaper, personifies the change as he abandons his muckrake
for a rifle; having accepted the priority of the war over reform,
he is killed in battle for his pains. Other characters are the
local banker's son, educated in Germany, who flirts with
treason; a German spy-saboteur who nearly succeeds in blow-

ing up the local munitions plant where he works as a chemist;
a couple of robber-baron industrialists who are reconstructed
into a belief in government regulation and safety measures
for workers as events of the novel unfold; Nancy Cowder,
the daughter of one of them, who at the end of the novel
is about to marry the Reverend Richard Ingraham, the youngish
minister whose Christian forebearance (as he educated his
fellow townsmen into a realization of their war responsibilities)
is faintly unbearable. Finally, high-spirited Patsy McCullon,
reminiscent of the author, comes from the town's middle class,
graduates from college, teaches school, is accepted by the
upper class in spite of it, marries Ralph, becomes pregnant
before he goes off to war, and responds with courage to his
death.

The plot of *The Rising of the Tide* is practically nonexistent,
the dialogue is stiff and unrealistic (Tarbell had a flair for
frontier dialect, as in her Lincoln country anecdotes, but not
for straight dialogue), and characterization is crude. The book
would be better described as a series of eleven feature articles
rather than as a novel. She herself commented that "it is not
a novel—only an attempt to put down in fictional form my
actual observations of what small town people thought and
felt about the coming and the cause of the great war. It has
small literary value but a certain historical value for those
who may in the future care to study the course of American
public opinion during the years covered."[8] Thus, with the
honesty which makes her disarming, Tarbell herself stated
what needs to be said about her "novel."

The controlling viewpoint of the story, which underlines
the prevailing social norms, is that of the local aristocrats who
are descendants of the English and the Scotch-Irish who had
settled in the area at about the time that the frontiersmen
described by Henry Adams were hacking their way through
the trans-Appalachian wilderness. They made their money in
land and then developed the town's coal mining and iron
industries which sustained its economy and aided the war
effort. The main ethnic character is Irish Katie Flaherty, the
faithful housekeeper of the Reverend Mr. Ingraham, who could
as well have been called Judy O'Grady. Following the usual
formula for the Irish, Tarbell portrays her as warm-hearted,
witty, mercurial, and, of course, lovable. Katie is lumbered

into line to advance the story when it transpires that she is the key figure in capturing the German spy, which she does to revenge her son killed in the war. Despite her impetuosity, Katie invariably addresses her employer as "Mr. Dick," for she also knows her place.

When Tarbell fails to mention *The Rising of the Tide* in *All in the Day's Work*, she indicates that her judgment of it was not favorable. The book was written before the Versailles conference that ended hopes for the just peace anticipated in the novel. The Versailles treaty demolished that hope just as the onset of the war had ended "the case against war" that she and David Starr Jordan had so hopefully set out to prepare. Perhaps disillusionment, added to the fact that it was a very bad novel, made her want to forget it. Nevertheless, the book is valuable Americana that is intelligently rendered. It manages to objectify at the very point of transformation the society Tarbell envisioned; it is not perfect, assuredly, but by implication it is perfectible. Never again would she see the components of that society acting together in dynamic harmony, as in the end they had come to do in *The Rising of the Tide;* for the 1920's would reveal the profound changes the war had wrought. Since Tarbell did not change with the times, though she had too much tolerant good sense to rail against change, she served as a stabilizing reminder of the traditional qualities which people in the 1920's told themselves had built American civilization. She was living proof in that squalid decade that those traits still existed.

Unlike Henry Adams, who in the end rejected the bright American Dream for a vision of darkest doom, Ida Tarbell retained the faith that a fighter must have in the worth of what he believes in. One of her sustaining basic beliefs was the unwavering conviction that mankind possesses the rationality and humanity to eliminate war. Although she had viewed from the start the entry of the United States into World War I as inevitable, Woodrow Wilson's vision, incorporated in the League of Nations, permanently reinforced her faith that "peace machinery" could rout forever the armaments of war. Shortly before Hitler's thrust into Poland in 1939, which precipitated World War II, she spoke for her belief: "If Peace is to displace War she can do it only by a machinery as scientific as is War's Navy, Army, Air Fleet, Fortifications. The machinery of Peace is diplomacy, a Hague Tribunal, A League of Nations, Peace Societies. They have proved inadequate, but are no more to be scrapped than an army defeated in the field. War re-organizes, re-equips his defeated Army. So must Peace her defeated machinery."[9]

Tarbell did not live to see either the machinery of peace reassembled as the United Nations or the erection of its headquarters in New York City, indicating that at last her countrymen had come to share her commitment to world cooperation as a source of peace. Nor did she live to learn of the atomic bombing of Hiroshima, an event which precipitated that commitment. Tarbell simplistically assigned to "War" the masculine gender and to "Peace" the feminine; war was conflict; peace, cooperation. The implied synthesis of this dialectic was peaceful conflict, as William James had recommended in 1910 when he suggested a "moral equivalent" for war that would channel the competitive energies of mankind into constructive social goals. Both James and Tarbell had assumed that human rationality would eventually prevail. That assumption, characteristic of the Progressive era, has since become more a desperate hope than a comforting surety. Yet that often forlorn hope at least remains as evidence of the heritage passed on by fighters like Tarbell and James.

III *Mussolini's Dimple*

After the Armistice, Tarbell returned to work, with John S. Phillips, her associate on *McClure's* and *The American*, who was now editor of the *Red Cross Magazine*, which had its headquarters in Paris. She eagerly returned to her favorite city and attempted to reestablish the friendships she had made there a quarter of a century before. The effort failed. Too much had happened since to make it possible to capture again the fine, heady flavor of the past. Many of the men were dead; the women were living dreary, deprived lives; and American ebullience did not sit well with them. Consequently, Tarbell turned to her work; there was plenty of that.

Phillips wanted her to cast a "fresh eye" on Red Cross rehabilitation efforts in France and report on them for the magazine. She traveled around France and everywhere met the incredible destruction resulting from the war. It seemed to her that the Red Cross could best help by donating to the

French the warehouses full of the "shirts, drawers, pajamas, scarfs, sweaters" made by American women's sewing circles for soldiers and never used. It must have seemed ironic to Tarbell to see concrete evidence of the results of her mobilizing women for the war effort stored in warehouses; it was as if the whole project had been designed merely to drain off excess energy and emotion. Determined to have the stores put to practical use, she devoted herself to the effort to have these garments distributed to people who really needed them. She demanded that "the Kalamazoo pajamas, the Topeka shirts, everybody's sweaters, . . . be refitted for children and men and women who at present have not a decent shirt to their backs, or decent drawers to their legs."[10] When she helped to organize distribution of the clothing, she was careful to leave it in the hands of the French, since it was their business, but to see that the distribution was wider and more efficient. She found it "consoling" to embark upon such a practical task.

Being an observer at the peace conference taxed her faith more than the devastation of the countryside, for there she had at least seen successful salvage efforts. "What startled me as the days went on," she recalled, "was the passing of the will to peace which had been strong, even taken for granted at the start. Hate was replacing it . . . the confusion and bitterness seemed daily more confounded."[11] However, she returned to the United States solaced that Wilson's League of Nations had been included in the treaty. She stumped the Northwest on a Chautauqua lecture tour in the summer of 1919 in support of the League—a forlorn effort to forestall the treaty's defeat by the Senate.

Wilson's health broke as he himself took to the country his unsuccessful plea for ratification of the Versailles treaty. To Tarbell, his tragedy was that he was ahead of his time; and she firmly believed that the future would bring his vindication. On the eve of World War II, she reiterated her faith:

He is the first leader in the history of civilization who has treated the ancient dream of a peaceful world as something more than wishful thinking, the first who was willing to stake all in drawing the nations of the world together in an effort to make that "just and lasting peace among ourselves and with all nations" for which Abraham Lincoln had pleaded. . . . The world will not forget the man who led this effort to achieve an enduring peace. That is what I was saying in those bitter days and have been saying in all the melancholy ones since.[12]

In this mood of discouragement Tarbell covered the Washington Disarmament Conference of 1921–22 for the McClure Syndicate. The resulting articles were published by Macmillan in 1922 and the book was entitled cynically, for her, *Peacemakers—Blessed and Otherwise: Observations, Reflections and Irritations at an International Conference.* The limitation of the conferees to representatives of only five nations—England, France, Japan, Italy, and the United States—seemed futile to Tarbell; and she did not trouble in her reports to veil her skepticism. She concluded her series with a pious though qualified hope: "The present conference has boldly and nobly attempted to do in a limited field something of what the Paris Conference attempted to do for the whole world. The limitation of armament it proposes rests, like world disarmament, on unionism, standing together. Unionism requires faith. Have we enough of it? It requires, too, men of good will. Have we enough of them? In the final analysis, it is with them that 'peace on earth' rests."[13]

Tarbell's disillusionment in the postwar world was widely shared; and, like that of many others, it was evidenced by a temporary infatuation with the Mussolini regime then coming to power in Italy. She marvelled at Mussolini's rescue of the nation from outright anarchy: to millions of Americans he was, for example, the wonder worker "who made the trains run on time." In 1926, when she was offered a large fee to write a series on her impressions of Italy, for *McCall's Magazine,* she decided to go despite the warnings of friends in Europe and of government officials that it was a risky enterprise. When she skimmed over the country in a four-month tour, all seemed peaceful, and Italians were at work. The warnings proved unsubstantiated, for she experienced no surveillance, she was not censored, and she was able to travel at will. She found the general attitude toward Mussolini one of, at worst, resigned acceptance of dictatorship rather than the previous chaos.

Finally, through the influence of Henry P. Fletcher, the American ambassador to Italy, she secured an interview with Mussolini. Reports of his brusque treatment of previous visitors had not prepared her for the gallantry of her reception. An animated half-hour was spent in talk about a topic of mutual interest, better housing for the poor. Despite her conviction that he was "a fearful despot," she was charmed by the unexpected discovery that the glowering Mussolini "had a dimple" when he smiled.[14] Presumably Mussolini also had an eye on good publicity.

After her return to the United States, Tarbell continued a sporadic correspondence with Italian propagandists. In 1932 she wrote an inquiry about the swift punishment Mussolini had decreed for an Italian speculator who had attempted to get rich at the expense of the Guild State. Mussolini had confiscated his assets, reimbursed investors, and given the speculator a five-year prison term. In the Guild State, Tarbell's informant explained, no private enterprise for individual gain was permitted. Tarbell replied, "I only wish we could deal with our financial adventurers in the fashion [Mussolini] did with this picturesque character. It would save us a world of trouble . . . [I am] reading your bulletins faithfully every month. It is certain that the Guild State is demonstrating more and more that it has something to offer tormented peoples. I am most anxious to get over again and check up on my former impressions."[15]

Her intention to return to Italy was probably more polite than actual, for she was aging, and her health began to fail. The most severe blow was the onset of Parkinson's disease; an unfortunate affliction in any case, it is peculiarly so for a writer. Tarbell had always written in longhand, but her hands became so palsied she could not write legibly at times; and she could not depend on the occurrence of remissions. Finally, she was forced to use a typewriter, working slowly and painfully. Only her determination made the switch in procedure possible, for it took her sometimes well over an hour to produce a page of typescript. In such fashion she fought off age and illness, for to her, work was life.

IV McClure's Attempts a Comeback

As though the record of her life were being played again, Tarbell received in 1921 a summons from S. S. McClure to help him bring back *McClure's* to its former glory. McClure, stubborn as ever, was determined to introduce readers of the

1920's to his magazine, put out in his own way. After Tarbell and the others had left in 1906 to take over *The American,* McClure had carried on a losing battle against declining circulation. In 1911, he was bought out; but he remained as titular editor unitl 1913. The war years saw a further decline as the public's tastes changed and as new magazines were created to meet them. In 1921, when *McClure's* went into bankruptcy, Moody B. Gates, a magazine editor and president of the F. M. Lupton Publishing Company, returned *McClure's* to solvency and installed McClure as editor. The first issue under his supervision appeared in March, 1921.

McClure's plan was to have Tarbell write for the magazine the third volume of her Standard Oil history and to concentrate on the current struggle between the Standard Oil Company and the Royal Dutch Shell Oil Company for control of the world petroleum trade. She replied to his summons at once, eager to get started on the project:

Before I die I must find time to bring the Standard Oil story up to date. What I contemplate begins with the suit [the government suit which resulted in the Supreme Court decision to dissolve the Standard Oil trust in 1911] itself and would be a pretty fine chapter in recent American history, Roosevelt himself being the central figure. Then comes the South West, and the immense efforts of the independents, free, as they suppose. There are remarkable chapters of struggle over new fields in different countries, and there is the story of how oil has become a governmental concern and the entry into the fight of governments. Altogether it is the material of which Oppenheim novels are made, only that most of the characters don't wear as good clothes or speak as many languages.... It is a prodigious piece of work and I would not undertake it until I had sufficient financial backing.[16]

Assured of an adequate subsidy, she set to work. But *McClure's* began to founder; and, by the time she had completed twenty thousand words of the Standard Oil history, McClure had purchased the magazine from Gates in a last hope of saving it. But nothing worked, and it folded in August. When McClure refused once more to give up, he attracted a backer, Lewis E. Myers, who wanted a magazine outlet to promote the toys he manufactured in Valparaiso, Indiana. Myers encouraged McClure to serialize a biography of Judge

Elbert H. Gary, chairman of the board of the United States Steel Corporation. According to Tarbell's own account, both in her autobiography and in the foreword to the Gary biography, published by D. Appleton and Company in 1925, the publishing company first approached her about writing it. Apparently she mentioned the offer to McClure and Myers, and Myers became an enthusiastic backer of the idea of using it as a circulation builder for *McClure's* new series. Myers's enthusiasm was logical, for big business had a glamor in the 1920's that exposés of its practices could not diminish.

Generous endorsements from old friends and admirers of McClure sprinkled the first of the new series of *McClure's*, the issue of May, 1925. Glenn Frank, editor of the *Century*, the magazine McClure had attempted to emulate in the early 1890's, said, "It was McClure who really democratized periodical literature for all of us." Will Irwin recalled that McClure was "the genius responsible for the modern American magazine." A reprint from the New York *Evening World* reminded readers that McClure had "discovered, introduced, or encouraged Joseph Conrad, Booth Tarkington, Conan Doyle, Jack London, and O. Henry." As for McClure's ambition, "The new *McClure's* has but one master, the Subscriber." The aim of the new series, according to his announcement, remained as protean as that of the old. It was, he declared "to deal with important social, economic and political questions; to present the new and great inventions and discoveries; to interpret the conquests of science; to advance great moral enthusiasms; to remove the barriers of the intellectual life; to promote the welfare of childhood and youth; to give the best in literature, and, above all to achieve an unforgettable charm and vitality in all its undertakings—all this is the aim of *McClure's*."

But few subscribers were any longer interested in such an all-inclusive aim, and rising young writers sought publication elsewhere. In the meantime, Tarbell had carefully considered the Gary biography and, after some preliminary reluctance, had agreed to write it. Myers's money was to keep the magazine afloat, and the hope was that Tarbell could work the same wonders with circulation that she had in the past. But Gary was a carefully dull and neutral Organization Man, the biography was consequently uninteresting to general readers, and the miracle of increased circulation did not occur. The first installment of the Gary biography was the lead article in the May, 1925, issue; and the final three chapters were jammed unceremoniously into the last one of the new series, the issue of January, 1926. As if to forestall *McClure's* imminent collapse, Appleton's published the completed biography prematurely in the fall of 1925. With the January issue Myers's money ran out, and McClure was forced to surrender. The subscriber so hopefully addressed less than a year before had rendered a verdict, and McClure finally had to accept it. The Hearst publications bought *McClure's,* and it became a sleazy romance magazine. The question remains as to whether McClure and his magazine were behind the times or too good for them. In the end, even Hearst could not revive it; in 1929, it was merged with the *Smart Set,* and *McClure's* was heard from no more.

CHAPTER *8*

Big Business Exonerated

I N 1939, fourteen years after publication of her biog-
graphy of Elbert H. Gary, Tarbell made an observation about him which is revealing about them both. The subject
was the image that Gary created after he had become a powerful
industrialist:

Judge Gary had done a great job, and he knew it; but, interestingly
enough, it never made him pompous. . . . Along with his really simple
enjoyment of his own conflict he had a nice kind of dignity and
a carefulness of conduct which were not entirely natural to him.
To be sure he had always been a good Methodist, a good citizen,
a hard-working lawyer; but at the same time he had led what was
then called a gay life. He had liked a fast horse, liked to hunt and
see the world. He was curious about all kinds of human performances,
looked into them whenever he had a chance. When he became the
head of the Steel Corporation he could no longer sing in the choir—he
had to go to the opera and sit in a box. He no longer drove fast
horses. He wanted to fly, and the board of the Steel Corporation
passed an ordinance against it—too dangerous. When he travelled
it was more or less in state, and he couldn't slip out with a crowd
of men at the stopping places to see the town.
  It was hard on him, but he felt deeply that he owed it to the Steel
Corporation to be above reproach. Not a little of this carefulness
was due, I think, to the effect on the public, the exhibits that several
of the new steel men had made of themselves after the Corporation
was formed in 1901 and their offices were centered in New York.
They were rich beyond their wildest dreams. The restrictions of the
home towns were gone, and they broke loose in a riotous celebration
which scandalized even Mr. [J. P.] Morgan. Gary joined in nothing
which approached orgies. He was too hard a worker and always had
been, and he saw with distress the effect the high living of certain
of the steel men was having on the public. It was a danger, he felt,
equal to the speculation in steel stock by officers of the corporation.
To counteract it he gradually became more and more a model of
correctness.[1]

  Part of Gary's image was the honorific title "Judge," a reminder of his service as part-time county judge of DuPage

County, Illinois, in the 1880's. The title carries with it certain Olympian connotations, but in Gary's case it seemingly had as much relevance to jurisprudence as that of "Kentucky Colonel" to the military profession. The next thing to note is the semantics of the word "pompous." In the passage above, Tarbell denies that Gary was pompous; but, to a reader, the description of Gary she provides might well make him sound so, since he is characterized by an ostentatious parade of dignity or importance. Why, for example, did Gary have to stop singing in a choir because he was head of United States Steel? Being head of the Standard Oil Company had not prevented John D. Rockefeller from continuing to teach Sunday School. And, though it is practically impossible to imagine J. P. Morgan wanting to sing in a choir, it is not at all difficult to conclude he would have done so if he had so desired. Why did the *nouveau riche* steel men's "orgies" scandalize "even" J. P. Morgan? One notes, too, how extremely conscious of public relations was the Judge. The whole description makes clear the commercialism of Victorian morality: be virtuous, not because it carries its own reward, but because it looks good, and *that* brings reward. Gary was, in effect, the prisoner of the corporation he headed—by courtesy of Morgan, as a matter of fact. If Morgan was a brutal, rapacious elitist, Gary was a pipsqueak potentate.

What Tarbell seems to be saying in the passage quoted is that, while Gary did indeed appear to be a pompous man, it was a disguise assumed to mask the joy of battle he thoroughly relished as he fought and clawed his way to the top. That, freely rendered, is what she seems to mean by putting in apposition Gary's "enjoyment of his own conflict" and a "dignity . . . not entirely natural to him." Since she genuinely approved of Gary, it seems valid to deduce that she approved not only of his creating an image but also of the image he created—that of the first Organization Man. Such men are artists in their own way. They are skilled in a rare accomplishment, the use of power. But, since love of power cannot be nakedly displayed in a bourgeois society, the image is necessary.

That both Gary and Tarbell obviously understood this fact shows them to be realists and also elitists. Both would have agreed they were realists, and doubtless both would quite sincerely have denied they were also elitists. No one can deny, though, that Tarbell set herself a difficult task in writing Gary's biography and in attempting to make it interesting. Proper Organization Man that he was, he had spent a considerable portion of his life avoiding being interesting. Wisely, she concentrated more on detailing the history of the steel industry than on that of Gary himself; for the biography was, in reality, a continuation of the history of American business that Tarbell had inaugurated with *The History of the Standard Oil Company*.

I   The Life of Elbert H. Gary: The Story of Steel

The thesis of *The Life of Elbert H. Gary* is clearly set forth in the preface to the book. Tarbell looked upon Gary, she explained, as one of the great shapers of big business; he was comparable to Rockefeller in oil, Morgan in banking, Harriman in railroads, Carnegie in steel. But he was so with a difference: he shared the eminence of these men, "not because he is the leader of the country's greatest industrial corporation, but chiefly because he has been a leader in developing a code of business practices, an attitude of mind radically at odds with that of the powerful at the time he became a factor to be reckoned with in the world."[2] From the first, she insisted, Gary had set himself against the dog-eat-dog code which had prevailed in industry and which he considered "impracticable" as well as "wrong." If Rockefeller had fathered bad trusts, Gary by implication had sired good ones. Indeed, the point of the biography is to demonstrate the latter proposition, as *The History of the Standard Oil Company* had established the former one.

Tarbell's basic empathy with Gary becomes immediately apparent in the biography as she describes his background, one so like her own. Like Lincoln's and her ancestors, Gary's had arrived early in New England, restlessly emigrated, and settled westward—in the Garys' case, near the Chicago area in 1831. Like Lincoln, Gary studied law; but, unlike Lincoln, he had useful family connections that enabled him, at the age of eighteen, to read law in his uncle's law office. After admission to the Illinois Bar, he married suitably and settled down in Wheaton. Gary did well from the first: he excelled in cross-examination, and he could extract from the most reluctant witnesses damaging admissions without seeming to draw blood. This ability was later to be helpful when he entered the industrial management arena. Gary's adroitness with witnesses, his biographer explains, stemmed from his belief that "a man can be a lawyer and still be a gentleman."[3]

As a corporation lawyer, Gary had been retained in 1898 by J. P. Morgan to supervise the establishment of the Federal Steel Company. He had completed his work and was ready to return home when Morgan, in his imperial manner, issued a decree informing him that he had been designated head of the new corporation. When Gary asked for time to consider, he was given twenty-four hours. In this confrontation, lion met fox; for Gary was a subtle man, equal in the end to the leonine Morgan. He accepted Morgan's offer—as well as Morgan's objective, which was to destroy the hold of Andrew Carnegie on the steel industry. By 1901, Gary had succeeded; and he was made chairman of the all-powerful executive committee of the newly formed United States Steel Corporation, which merged Carnegie's holdings and those of many of the lesser iron and steel companies.

Gary thus became the vice-regent of an industrial empire ruled by Morgan. The public was alarmed when it learned of the formation of this first billion-dollar corporation. Gary, who was conscious of the negative public reaction to United States Steel, feared its effect. Charles M. Schwab, one of the early "the public be damned" industrialists, had been made president of the corporation; and a power struggle between him and Gary began. Morgan backed Gary; Schwab was replaced in 1903 by another former Carnegie partner, W. E. Corey; and Gary's title was changed to that of chairman of the board. With Tarbell's usual finesse, she foreshadowed her conclusion and implemented her thesis by means of her description of the struggle between Schwab and Gary.

Just before the announcement of the formation of the United States Steel Corporation was released to the press, Morgan had asked his lawyers' opinions about its legality. All of them but Gary reassured him; Gary, who delivered a carefully qualified opinion, replied:

I believe, Mr. Morgan, that if there should be a direct attack by the Attorney-General against the new corporation at the beginning of its business career, the attack would probably be successful for the reason that so large a percentage of the iron and steel business is included in the new company; as the intentions of the organization have not been demonstrated, the Corporation is liable to be held to be a monopoly in opposition to the Sherman law. But I also think that if the Corporation with its business is properly managed and is allowed to continue in business until it has been proven that the intentions of the managers are good, that there is no disposition to exercise a monopoly or to restrain legitimate trade, that in that case, if there is a contest, the company will be held legal.[4]

To underscore her point in including Gary's meticulous analysis, Tarbell added: "This little speech to Mr. Morgan is vastly more important than it may look to the general reader. It is the first announcement, so far as I know, of a classification of trusts which was to become famous in the next few years —good and bad trusts."[5]

In depicting the contrast between the bad old days and the good new ones—personified by the struggle between Schwab and Gary—and in ascribing the importance she does to supple Gary's "little speech" to Morgan, Tarbell shows that she was herself fascinated by the power politics of business, of which Gary proved himself a consummate master. She probably overestimated the degree of his moral commitment, which she felt must be inseparable from business, as from all else. However that may be, Gary seems to have exceeded considerably any moral commitment that his predecessors possessed, and evidently enough to satisfy Tarbell that he was one of the "good guys."

Tarbell deals forthrightly with the labor problems of United States Steel, but invariably from the management standpoint. The Homestead strike of 1892 had crippled rising union power and left behind it ferocious hostility between management and labor. In 1901, when labor unrest threatened once again to boil over, the corporation flatly forbade any extension of union activity. In spite of this fiat, the Amalgamated Association of Iron, Steel, and Tin Workers called a strike in the tin plate industry, a subsidiary of United States Steel, when the workers' demands were not met. When the strike failed in winning support because most workers were unorganized, it was canceled within two months. The industry worked actively against unionization by instituting measures designed to pacify the workers, and by announcing two cardinal principles: open shops must be maintained; excepting for the few weak unions in existence when the corporation was formed in 1901, no negotiations would be entered upon with any union. That policy, Tarbell remarked, "has never been changed from that day to this."[6]

As she explained approvingly, a profit-sharing plan was inaugurated in 1903. Employees were encouraged to invest a certain proportion of their earnings in stock. For example, an employee earning eight hundred dollars a year could invest up to 20 percent of that sum and payments would be deducted from his wages. Moreover, "if he kept the stock, remained with the company and showed proper interest in its welfare," he would be entitled to a premium of five dollars a year for five years.[7] Just what "proper interest" toward the corporation's welfare might be was not specified, but it is doubtful that union activity would have been so construed. The stock, it so happened, depreciated in value in 1904 and was renamed "the loss-sharing plan" by the workers, few of whom could afford to participate in the plan anyway. Tarbell was too honest a reporter to deny that the profit-sharing plan was not well received by the majority of the corporation's employees, who would have preferred more wages and fewer hours. But she approved of the plan in principle, for she shared the common belief of her class that only the shiftless would fail to participate, and the fault was, of course, theirs.

The story of Gary's relationship with the reform-minded government of Theodore Roosevelt reveals the discontentment of his peers of the old robber-baron persuasion with what they considered his weak accommodation to the idea of government regulation of industry. Despite their vociferous disapproval, Gary cooperated with Roosevelt and government regulatory agencies. Consequently, he was dismayed when Congress in 1905 ordered an investigation of United States Steel on the ground it was a monopoly; but Gary continued to defend Roosevelt against the attacks of his unreconstructed colleagues. The investigation took several years; and, when it was concluded, James R. Garfield, who conducted the investigation for the United States Bureau of Corporations, reported to Roosevelt that, "compared to what he was discovering in other corporations, the Steel Corporation is a good trust."[8] Garfield's definition of a "good" trust, and presumably Tarbell's also, is thus seen to be a relative one. It must be remembered, however, that her onward and upward evolutionary view would have caused her to postulate that more improvements were bound to follow the first ones instituted by Gary.

The internecine conflict within the corporation continued. But Gary had remained close to Morgan, and in 1910, to end another power struggle, was enabled to consolidate clearly and unequivocally his powers as chairman of the board. As an example of his conciliatory philosophy of management, Tarbell recounted an interview she had had with him in 1908 when she was writing *The Tariff in Our Times*. He was, he frankly admitted, a believer in protective tariffs; but he added a qualification: he thought it was useless to contest downward tariff revision; for, in the matter of the tariff, "as in all others, public opinion was the true guide." Sound tariff revision, he said, the point beyond which protection became venal prohibition of foreign competition, should be established by neutral experts, not by politicians.[9] Since Gary's interview with Tarbell occurred shortly before passage of the Payne-Aldrich Tariff Bill of 1909, a reader might easily conclude that Gary was able to ingratiate himself with Tarbell at no expense, since the tariff now became the highest ever. Nevertheless, Tarbell retained her conviction that, for an industrialist, Gary's tariff views were enlightened.

The labor policy of United States Steel was by 1910 firmly established. The open shop was mandatory; profit-sharing was optional; safety measures were increasing; compensation and pension funds were growing; and the work week had been cut from seven to six twelve-hour days a week. Samuel Gompers, according to Tarbell, "characterized the program as a sham." She, on the other hand, believed in the good intentions of the corporation, and accepted without question the paternalism of its labor policy. "It was a policy that, for any degree of success," she cautioned, "required faith and cooperation on the part of the worker."[10] She seemingly never understood that the dignity of labor embraces in the minds of most workers more self-determination than is involved in company handouts, however well intentioned. In her view, while women should rock the cradle, labor by the same token should not rock the boat.

In 1911, the government dissolved the Standard Oil Trust and the Tobacco Trust. Another suit was begun in 1912 against United States Steel for violation of the Sherman Anti-Trust Act, and it continued for two years. In 1914, when the conflict in Europe became general, the national interest took precedence over the law suit against an industry which was vital to the United States. For all practical purposes, the corporation was exonerated; and it again resumed its place among the "good" trusts. While its antiunion policies were continued, Gary had come so far as to admit the merits of company unions. Company towns were built, and social services to workers and their families were extended. In Gary, Indiana, named in honor of the head of United States Steel, the company schools followed the progressive educational methods of John Dewey and were widely praised by advanced educators and by the liberal community. Randolph Bourne, who in 1915 had not yet abandoned Dewey and the liberal pragmatists over the issue of American entry into the war, wrote an excellent, highly laudatory series of articles about the Gary schools for the *New Republic*.

The suit against the steel corporation which had been dropped in 1914 was reactivated in 1917, but was again tabled. In 1919, it was resumed; and the corporation was finally exonerated of the charges against it. Tarbell wrote, "The government had lost its suit. The 'good' trust had won as Judge Gary always contended it would."[11] One of Gary's associates earnestly assured her that Gary had "put the Golden Rule in the Steel Corporation's business,"[12] and she found no reason to disagree. She realized that her defense of Gary would incur the wrath of liberals, and she once remarked that it was the only book she ever wrote that demanded courage to publish.[13] She rested her case on two main assumptions: first, that so-called good trusts are desirable; second (and more debatable), that Gary's labor policies were progressive. She was convinced that both assumptions were correct.

The Life of Elbert H. Gary is well written. For dramatic tension Tarbell contrasted Gary's theory that good trusts would be accepted by the government with the series of government suits which tested it. Personal drama arose from her description of the intense power struggle between the enlightened Gary and adherents of unreformed corporate practices, such as

Charles M. Schwab. The struggle between the two men for control of United States Steel culminated in 1903 with Schwab's resignation as president of the corporation and with Gary firmly in control. The personality of the elder Morgan, which is briefly but effectively projected, provides a welcome relief to the grayness of Gary himself. In her conclusion Tarbell conferred upon Gary the title "Industrial Statesman" for his achievements in socializing big business. Her case is solid and well constructed; there can be no doubt that she believed in it and in him.

II The Critics

In retrospect, perhaps the most interesting thing about publication of *The Life of Elbert H. Gary* is the critical response to the book in the liberal press; a clear generation gap between Tarbell and her critics became apparent. For in the Gary biography Tarbell's facts were, as always, scrupulously accurate. As in the case of *The History of the Standard Oil Company*, the differences among critics occurred in the matter of emphasis and interpretation; and the liberal critics seized upon her defense of Gary's labor policies. Allan Nevins's review of the book in the New York *World*, while more moderate in tone than most, nevertheless indicates the deep division between the postwar liberals, who were pro-labor in sympathy, and prewar liberals, like Tarbell, who favored management. Their quarrel had not been with private enterprise as such but with special privilege. In Nevins's opinion, Gary's "hostility toward collective bargaining, his long hesitancy to attempt abolition of the twelve-hour day ... cannot but remain a reproach to his 'industrial statesmanship.' Miss Tarbell's *ex parte* history of this aspect of the career of Judge Gary and his corporation is the one glaring defect in an able and engrossing work."[14]

An earlier, unsigned review in the same newspaper, "The Taming of Ida M. Tarbell," accused her of deserting the left, as well as her function as a liberal of attacking the status quo in order to prevent society from falling into indolent self-complacency. "One wishes," remarked the reviewer, "that she had let somebody else place the laurel on Judge Gary's brow."[15] This reviewer was disappointed in Tarbell, and his reaction had been one that she had particularly dreaded. For she stood high among liberals, mostly on the strength of her Standard Oil history but also as a result of her usually predictable stands on social questions. However, the *World* reviewer would not have been so disappointed had he recalled Tarbell's opposition to feminism. Although Tarbell considered herself a liberal, she and other Muckrakers of the Progressive era were usually accused of having joined the establishment by critics and historians of the 1920's, 1930's, and 1940's. By then only Progressives who had advocated Socialism were still permitted under the umbrella of "liberalism"; for, after Lenin, their Socialism seemed pale pink enough to be classified as liberal; indeed, it seemed quaint to Marxists of the 1930's.

But the liberal Muckrakers had been against the establishment and had dedicated themselves to toppling it. The oligarchy established by Rockefeller, Morgan, Harriman, and the rest of the first wave of post-Civil War industrialists had been their target; and they had succeeded in helping trim their power and in forcing the early industrialists to operate within the law. Agree or not, a corporation like Gary's must have seemed marvelous after those Tarbell had known in the nineteenth century. To the next generation of liberals, United States Steel was the establishment to be fought; to her, it represented victory—and the Gary biography celebrated that victory. At the same time, she must have know that she would no longer be considered a relevant social critic by younger writers; but Tarbell was not one to occupy a pedestal under false pretenses.

Benjamin Stolberg, *The Nation*'s critic, took another tack in his review entitled "St. Elbert and the Heavenly Trust" by calling the Gary biography sheer fantasy. He conceded that *The History of the Standard Oil Company* remained "the most outstanding attack against the Machiavelli of Big Business"; furthermore, he disagreed that *The Life of Elbert H. Gary* represented a sellout of principle by its author. After noting that she had always been friendly to big business, he theorized that *The History of the Standard Oil Company* had been a work of filial revenge caused by Rockefeller's ruination of her father. Her consequent hatred of Standard Oil, wrote Stolberg, "developed in her a sort of suppressed desire for a fairy trust," and this desire had been fulfilled by Gary's steel corporation. Stolberg insisted that J. P. Morgan was the

actual founder of United States Steel and that Gary was a
"Babbitt Buddha, . . . among the first to discover that one must
never say 'the public be damned,' but say 'the public be
served.' The difference—and therein lies our hero's discovery—is very slight; and it pays. Miss Tarbell's saint is also
the patron saint of Rotaria."[16] Aside from revealing the twin
influences of Freud and Sinclair Lewis, Stolberg's review provides insight into the shift of liberals away from defense of
middle-class values. Tarbell and the Progressives had
defended those values against the encroachment of the
oligarchs; but postwar critics were intent upon destroying that
same "Puritan" value system which they viewed as a threat
to American society.

Tarbell still spoke for the average, middle-class American,
however, just as she had in her history of Standard Oil. For
in the Harding and Coolidge eras big businessmen were
popular heroes, and the public read and believed their statements that corporations were designed primarily to serve the
community first, and only secondly to make money. *The Life
of Elbert H. Gary* is perfectly consistent, then, with Tarbell's
attitudes toward business and labor. Her younger critics who
were pro-labor were adamantly opposed to the value system
upheld by the "Babbitt" Gary.

What her critics probably meant to imply is that she had
been co-opted by the corporation, perhaps through the very
availibility of their records which added a degree of complexity
to her evaluation that had not been present when she wrote
The History of the Standard Oil Company and when her
sources had been largely court documents and other adversary
material. In addition, her critics failed to take into account
that she was a veteran of the era when trusts were first devised
and their practices were absolutely unregulated; whereas they
were generally of the next generation which looked upon the
second wave of industrialists, or men like Gary, much as she
had regarded the first wave. And it seems logical that she
would view with favor a man who, like Gary, bowed to government regulation and to the regulatory power of the press; for
these were the very things Tarbell had worked for and had
been instrumental in securing. The sweet fruits of her victory
in the battle of her lifetime had been the Supreme Court decision in 1911 dissolving the Standard Oil Trust. As for criticism

of her apparent concurrence with Gary's labor policy, it was more real that apparent; for Tarbell was management oriented. Her attitude toward labor was similar to her response to militant feminism; labor, like women, was assigned a subsidiary role in her scheme for the good society.

Finally, how could the author of *The Golden Rule in Business* disapprove of a man of whom it could be said that he had applied that very Rule to the largest corporation in the country?

III *Old Soldiers Never Die*

By the 1930's, the mass of Tarbell's Lincoln source material had been exhausted, producing only an occasional article or folksy sidelight; but Tarbell's interest in Lincoln continued unabated. In the spring of 1939, where she taught a seminar in biography to students at Allegheny College, she used as resource material her own large Lincoln collection, which she had recently donated to the college. She emphasized in the course the importance of biography as a branch of history and literature, and she stressed also her conviction that biography should be an effective "guide to the management of one's own life." In addition, the course aimed to bring out the humanity of Lincoln—to show that he was not a saint, nor merely a hero, but "all man." She told her students that of all his qualities, the "most impressive had been his mastery of his own nature," for his had been "a story of continued growth. Something larger comes out of every period, something more than he started with."

The students were charmed by her lively interest in everything and everybody.[17] They shared the response of a reporter who interviewed her that spring after publication of her autobiography. The reporter noticed particularly that her eyes were lively and that their constant change of expression was the focus of interest in her face. When the conversation turned to muckraking, Tarbell said she preferred to be known as a "student of the times" rather than as a Muckraker. On women's suffrage, her attitude had remained constant: "People thought women would improve politics because they were better. It isn't so. Women aren't better, they're different." She admitted she could tolerate women's suffrage but was largely indifferent to it. She thought women should stay home and raise families because they are the source of good democracy.[18]

Very likely her students at Allegheny College responded to her capacity for exploration and growth, the quality whose worth she had learned from Lincoln. The title of her autobiography, *All in the Day's Work,* had not been idly chosen. To her, work was growth; she never stopped writing. Occasionally, she mentioned in a letter a favorite plan, never carried out, to write about an island utopia. Among her papers is a complete outline for a study of old age to be called *Life After Eighty.* The proposed study of age, the outline indicated, was to stress the need to reevaluate oneself at eighty and to reorder one's aims and objectives. The final section was to attempt to answer the question "How useful can a fifth score be made?"[19]

Ray Stannard Baker found in his official biography of Woodrow Wilson and in the editing of Wilson's letters a fourteen-year task which became the sustaining major work of his later years. Although no project of that magnitude fell to Tarbell, she had always on hand a number of assignments; indeed, she was offered more than she could take on. In 1934, when she was asked by the Edward Bellamy Association to write a biography of Bellamy, she rejected the offer, partly, she replied, because, although she felt he had made a great contribution to American thought, she was no "Bellamite."[20] The request produced instead an article for *The Forum,* "New Dealers of the 'Seventies: Henry George and Edward Bellamy." The article pointed out the continuity between the work of George's, Bellamy's, and Franklin D. Roosevelt's New Deal; and compared unfavorably the hurried improvisation of Roosevelt's New Deal with the carefully worked out theories of the earlier men, "the like of whose voices has not been heard in the present turmoil."[21]

IV   Owen D. Young: A New Type of Industrial Leader

In 1931, Tarbell began the last volume in her trilogy about big business. Her unique distinction is to have written, as a contemporary, histories of business in three successive waves of development, an accomplishment that was compatible with her preference for ordered progression. Her biography of Owen D. Young, chairman of the board of the General Electric Company and famed reparations "troubleshooter" for the United States during the 1920's, rounded out the cycle begun with the originator of big business, John D. Rockefeller. Her three studies of the evolution of business thus include the first amoral exploiters, represented by Rockefeller; their successors, whose model was Gary, the builder of a "good" trust; and Young, who represents the ideal of industry in social service. How close Young approached her ideal is evidenced by the uncritically eulogistic treatment he receives in the biography. Tarbell seems to have been trapped, even more in Young's case than in Gary's, by her own dream of socialized, capitalistic industry as a pattern of democracy, into a euphoria which seems highly unrealistic to those who do not share it.

In her foreword she defended herself in advance against the reviewers by admitting that she had written "what approaches a eulogy" and by explaining that the enthusiasm of Young's associates for him had added to her own. "After all," she continued, half apologetic and half defiant, "I have never been one who felt that the praise of him you believe to be a good man is a shame to a writer, any more than I have felt the condemnation of a man you believe evil is a particular virtue in a writer. A biographer's business is to set down as faithfully as he can what he finds and that I have tried to do in writing this sketch of Owen D. Young."[22] Unfortunately, overenthusiasm is usually fatal to a biography; consequently, the Young biography forms a very weak concluding volume for Tarbell's trilogy of business. At the same time, it is a strong affirmation of her acceptance of the dominance of what she considered benevolent big business in American affairs—an attitude that sharply contrasts with her condemnation of the malignant influence of the carly trusts.

Old habits die hard: Tarbell was wedded to the practice of serialization before publication as a means of increasing her income from a book. Serialization of the Gary biography in *McClure's* had been a fiasco, yet she turned hopefully to another familiar periodical, *The American*, for serialization of the Young biography. An announcement in that journal duly promised that a biography of Owen D. Young, written by Ida M. Tarbell, would appear in coming issues. The first installment appeared in the issue of October, 1931, and was followed by a notice that the next would appear in November; but none appeared. Instead, a short article by Tarbell about Young's theories of education was carried in *The American*'s issue of February, 1932. That she was nevertheless busily at work was

soon evidenced by publication of the completed biography
by Macmillan early in the summer of 1932. The book was
entitled *Owen D. Young: A New Type of Industrial Leader.*
The book recounted the rise of the third generation of industrialists, exemplified by Young, a shaper of the managerial
revolution. Born in 1874, Young had ventured beyond Gary's
"industrial statesmanship" into international government service as a result of his skill as an industrial administrator. He
had helped formulate the Dawes Reparations Plan for Germany, and also the plan, named for him, which replaced the
Dawes Plan. His record of public service was long and brilliant
and it marked a return to the original Puritan ideal of
stewardship, in the estimation of observers like Ida Tarbell.

Young came from old Protestant American stock. His ancestors had left the Palatinate in the seventeenth century to escape
Catholic persecution, had eventually emigrated to America
with other Palatine religious refugees early in the eighteenth
century, and had settled in Western New York, where they
served as a buffer against hostile Indians for the English who
had permitted them to settle there. Like the Rockefellers, who
had produced the anomalous John D., the Youngs quickly
became assimilated into the dominant culture.

Son of a farmer in modest circumstances, Young early
showed promise as a student and dislike of the incessant, grind-
ing work of farming. To become a lawyer, he studied at Boston
University Law School after Harvard had refused him; and
he was graduated *cum laude* in 1896 after two years instead
of the usual three. He then entered a Boston law firm and
taught law at Boston University. Before very long he began
the corporate career in which he became internationally recognized as a top industrialist and as head of General Electric.
Unlike most industrialists, however, Young was a Democrat.
How much that fact had to do with the genesis of Tarbell's
biography in a presidential election year is a matter of conjec-
ture, though many thought the connection was close. Certainly
the biography of Young dwelt far more on him and his personal
achievements than on the history of the utilities business,
while the approach had been the opposite in both *The History
of the Standard Oil Company* and *The Life of Elbert H. Gary.*
Certainly the suspicion of E. J. Hopkins, who reviewed the
Young biography in the *New Republic,* July 20, 1932, that

"the Democratic National Convention was to have written the book's final chapter after publication, and didn't" cannot be dismissed as improbable. Young had been mentioned as a possible candidate for governor of New York in 1925, had been touted by the New York *Times* for the Democratic nomination for the presidency in 1928, and again was widely considered as a possibility for the nomination in 1932.

There is little reason to doubt that Tarbell would have welcomed Young's candidacy in 1932, but apparently no documentary evidence exists to show that she did. She had not supported Herbert Hoover, another business candidate, in 1928, because he was a Republican. By 1939 even this bias disappeared when she supported Wendell Willkie and turned away from Roosevelt because of his unprecedented bid for a third term.

V *Ida Tarbell and the New Deal*

Ida Tarbell's admiration for Lincoln did not extend to the Republican party as she had come to know it after the Civil War. She had become a Democrat when Cleveland became President, had deserted that party when the too radical William Jennings Bryan had been its presidential candidate, and had returned to it with Wilson. She supported Alfred E. Smith's candidacy, despite her personal liking for Hoover and her respect for his ability. She felt Hoover's strength was in smoothing relationships between government and business but that Smith was a politician who excelled in "the applied science of government." Moreover, because she suspected that Hoover was too attached to the status quo, Smith appealed to her as an innovator who always looked before he leapt. These assessments, expressed in an interview with Smith for *Collier's*, one similar to that in 1916 with Woodrow Wilson for the same magazine, very accurately indicate her stance on social questions as somewhere between conservative and liberal: progressive conservative perhaps defines her best.

As was the case in the Wilson interview, that with Governor Smith faithfully records her position about her favorite issues and only incidentally records Smith's. The Republicans of fifty years before, she wrote, echoing *The Tariff in Our Times*, had made an alliance with the manufacturers, and these became members of a favored caste, as had factory workers in Russia under the Communists. Reverting to the issue of public resources, another Tarbell favorite, she claimed that 80 percent of the electric power in the United States was controlled by private companies—and 50 pecent of that by five companies—because of Republican policies. Smith and the Democrats, she asserted, opposed these policies; they believed that the people should have control of their own power resources. "It is not big and efficient business that Governor Smith and his party condemn," she explained, "it is business founded on special interests, on private control of powers which belong to the state. What he and his party are against is class government, which is a very different thing from business government."[23]

"Centralized wealth breeds arrogance," she scolded, which engenders consequent disregard for the public interest. The Democratic party sought to decentralize wealth and to increase popular control of it, she declared. On the indelicate subject of Smith's Tammany ties, she sniffed that "the country had better be Tammanyized than Harry Sinclairized."[24] Her agreement with the Democrats about the tariff prompted her to remark that she shared their conviction that "tariff-made prosperity" cannot be evenly distributed. In this respect her central divergence from Hoover becomes evident, for she vehemently disagreed with his tariff creed. He "honestly believes protection to be the cause of prosperity," she contended.

In Tarbell's discussion of two delicate problems in Smith's candidacy—his Catholicism and his anti-Prohibition stand —she reached back to the Founding Fathers to remind her readers that freedom of religion was guaranteed by the Bill of Rights. Having settled that thorny problem expeditiously, she quickly disposed of the other. She shared Smith's negative view of Prohibition, she said, because it was an invasion of another guarantee, sanctioned by the Declaration of Independence: the right to personal liberty. To Tarbell, the cause of the failure of Prohibition to work effectively was resentment of it by the majority of Americans. And last, she invoked her reverence for the masses from which Smith had emerged in approved Tarbellian fashion. For "it all comes down to how much faith we have in the mass. For myself," she intoned, "I feel with Governor Smith that democracy is so eternally right that Almighty God is our strength."[25] Despite having Tarbell and God on his side, Smith lost; and Hoover swept to an easy victory on the wings of business (and prejudice).

From that point, Tarbell ceased to speak for the majority. She had not changed, but the times had gone beyond her, and she was now a living memory; soon annual interviews on her birthday would become a feature of leading newspapers. These were invariably interesting, for she was, in her under-played way, a salty old lady and a game one. The masses left her for Hoover; later, enthusiastic about Roosevelt, they deserted her as she remained cool about the New Deal. It seems ironic that the New Deal, which carried out many of the reforms first broached in the Progressive era, failed to gain Tarbell's wholehearted assent. But she could never abide rapid, chaotic change; nor could she tolerate this Roosevelt's unpredictability that was so reminiscent of his cousin who had preceded him as President.

Shortly before publication of Tarbell's biography of Owen D. Young, George Creel, whom she had known since their muckraking days, asked Tarbell if he could add her name to a list of fifty writers who were endorsing Roosevelt for the presidency. Her response was unfavorable, for she had no high opinion of his qualifications. Though she favored the Democratic party, she felt that Roosevelt's approach to economic reconstruction was superficial. In addition, she disliked his apparently low opinion of the League of Nations. Although she even considered voting for that perennial beneficiary of protest votes, Norman Thomas, the Socialist candidate, she did support Roosevelt.[26]

She had quite naturally always resented Theodore Roosevelt's unexpected slap in the face when in 1906 he had labelled those who had aided him so valiantly as "muckrakers." Very probably both Roosevelts' aristocratic origins alienated her somewhat; for as has been noted, her mystique of democracy was Emersonian in that she believed great leaders emerge from the mass of the people and represent their peoples' greatness. She had, at the same time, warm admiration for Eleanor Roosevelt, that marvelous woman, in whom her sex forgave greatness, perhaps because her beauty was of the inner variety. Notably, all the men Tarbell admired—Lincoln, her father, McClure, Phillips, Wilson, Gary, Young—had come, by and large, from the white, Anglo-Saxon, Protestant mass —the masses of the dominant ethnic group; and most were Midwesterners, as she considered herself to be.

Toward the end of Franklin Roosevelt's first term, Tarbell

found herself in agreement with Walter Lippmann, who
charged that Roosevelt acted impulsively in grave matters,
"as if government was a matter of gay improvisation." Like
Lippmann, she favored many New Deal measures in principle;
but she objected to their sloppy planning and messy execution.
She thought that Roosevelt's bias was essentially aristocratic,
that his handling of the National Recovery Administration had
been highly autocratic, and revealed his "weakness . . . in a
democratic government as well as anything. It [the National
Recovery Administration] was an assumption of authority obviously outside the law. It is well that the Supreme Court has
reminded him by its decision [the National Recovery Administration was declared unconstitutional in 1935] that he went
beyond the law and that cannot be done in a democratic
country."

Tarbell stated that she doubted that wages and hours could
be regulated from Washington, as the National Recovery
Administration proposed. She also defended the legitimacy
of company unions and was opposed to the closed shop, which
was currently being advocated by the rising Congress of Industrial Organizations; and her reason was that the closed shop
relied on majority rule! Returning to the topic of the National
Recovery Administration decision, she remarked that "the Supreme Court is as useful an instrument in a democracy as
a good brake on a car."[27]

In comments provoked by yet another Lippmann column
that year, she declared that she was not against the New Deal;
for, in spite of its often "misdirected energy," it was better
than "the inaction which preceded it." She counted as solid
gains of the Roosevelt administration the repeal of "the Prohibition mistake," the Social Security legislation, and the laws
designed to prevent the speculation which had hastened the
Depression.[28]

The lack of apparent rationale; the rapidity of change:
Roosevelt's unpredictability; the rise of union power, as great
a threat, she feared, as the once unregulated power of the
early industrialists, were Tarbell's major objections to the New
Deal. The rise of an autocracy in Italy had interested her,
and she had treated it tolerantly. But the slightest hint of it
in the United States in a President who "went beyond the
law and that cannot be done in a democratic country" was

another matter entirely. Her response leads an observer to conclude that she almost believed democracy was an American invention.

Yet she did not become bitter. Autobiography, no matter how guarded, is very revealing. While Tarbell's, written in the late 1930's, is selective in providing glimpses of her personal life, it does not seem guarded; nor is it self-serving beyond the perfectly understandable desire to inch her best foot forward on occasion. If the work is in part an *apologia*, it is a fair and unimpassioned one that reveals a personality of great strength behind a balanced tolerance and genuine unpretentiousness, a combination which gracefully complements an equally genuine but unassertive worldly wisdom. *All in the Day's Work* makes clear to a reader exactly what Baker meant when he said that Tarbell was beautiful with virtue.

VI   The Nationalizing of Business, 1878–1898

In 1936, Tarbell's last major book, aside from the autobiography, was published; but it had been in fitful progress for thirteen years. An account of the era which produced her greatest book, *The History of the Standard Oil Company, The Nationalizing of Business, 1878–1898* is reminiscent of the earlier work only as the distant rumble of thunder signals the surly departure of a recent storm. She had never liked the assignment and had laid it aside time and time again for a more lucrative or interesting one. Since there is no reference to it in her autobiography, she evidently did not consider it worthy of inclusion. By no means a bad book, it remains a highly competent contribution to the distinguished twelve-volume series *A History of American Life,* each volume by a specialist in the periods ranging from 1492 to the the 1920's and edited by Arthur M. Schlesinger and Dixon Ryan Fox. Hers, the ninth volume, furnishes an overview of the transformation of American business which took place during these two decades.

The main reason writing the book did not appeal to her was that the fee was excessively modest for the amount of work involved. *A History of American Life,* while designed with general readers in mind, did not expect a wide audience outside the colleges and universities; and Tarbell, a thoroughly professional journalist, measured success in sales, not in scholarly kudos. In addition, she felt uncomfortable doing the book. The format of the series cramped her; the panoramic scope of her project went against her inclinations, for she excelled in illuminating the general through particulars, as when she had focused on John D. Rockefeller and the Standard Oil Company in order to delineate the changes in business. Furthermore, her specialty was the feature story, not abstract theoretical analysis. Moreover, she felt insecure in the company of academic historians of already considerable reputation, though some were comparatively young. The day had passed when amateurs and professional historians labored side by side; for, with the burgeoning of the social sciences, academic historians had become convinced that history classified as a social science would prosper and become more respected in the academy than if it remained merely an art which any good writer could practice if he so desired.

The overtures to secure her consent to do the book had come in 1923 from Authur Schlesinger, for he was to write the companion volume to *The Nationalizing of Business, The Rise of the City, 1878–1898*. His book would be a cultural history of the period whose economy Tarbell's volume would cover. Tarbell was not enthusiastic; but, when he persisted, she finally agreed to sign a contract. The deadline she and the editors agreed on was February, 1925. Two years seemed a long time in such affairs, but delay followed delay, apology followed apology. Schlesinger remained patient throughout and he was finally rewarded by receipt of a manuscript.[29]

In the editors' foreword to *The Nationalizing of Business*, they stressed its relevance to the 1930's. Tarbell's volume, they said, presented a "picture of the sweep of American economic development—its freshness, its vitality, its lack of moral scruple."[30] They lauded her as "the foremost authority on the earliest and greatest of the industrial trusts," and they praised *The Tariff in Our Times* for its original insight into "the relation of pressure groups to tariff making." Her subject in *The Nationalizing of Business* was, the editors explained, "the building of a continent-wide economy" which, they pointed out, had produced problems not yet resolved: "The maldistribution of wealth, the paradox of poverty amidst plenty, the fluctuation of the business cycle, the tug of war between capital and labor, the unequal position of the farmer in the national economy, the danger to a democratic society of vast economic power vested in irresponsible hands."[31] The almost frenzied liveliness of tone in the foreword, with its now all-too-familiar argument of relevance, seems almost calculated to offset the unexciting documentation in the book itself. For, while Tarbell avoided leaping to conclusions, she painfully plodded to all too many.

Her book was limited to what is known as "the dismal science," economics. The term "business" includes all aspects of industrialism, including labor and farming. The treatment is densely factual, abstract, and of necessity largely impersonal; but the author works in dialogue when the opportunity offers. A reader familiar with Tarbell's interests detects a prime one immediately: Abraham Lincoln is evoked as he might have viewed a postwar nation "he hardly would have recognized and of which he could scarcely have approved."[32] The volume concludes with a judgment by Henry Demarest Lloyd on the snares of an unregulated *laissez-faire* economy: "Our civilization has followed the self-interest of the individual to learn that it was but one of the complex forces of self-interest. The true *laissez-faire* is, let the individual do what the individual can do best, and let the community do what the community can do best."[33] The need for Loyd's preachment is underlined by Tarbell's closing reminder that, at the end of the nineteenth century, "Carnegie's strong man still occupied the saddle" and showed no disposition to dismount.

In between the symbolic figures of Lincoln and Andrew Carnegie Tarbell included accounts of the spread of population throughout the continent and into the cities, the rise of labor organizations, farm problems, transformations wrought by continental railroads, and the conflict in ideologies between upholders of classical economics and those who argued passionately for social-welfare legislation and for government regulation of business. The book as a whole is informative, and it manages to convey a sense of the trends of the era being woven together in the loom of history.

The final chapter, conforming to the general format of the series, is an excellent critical essay about source materials. For this chapter, and for technical assistance generally, Tarbell expressed in correspondence with Schlesinger gratitude to her research assistant W. C. Langsam, then a young Columbia University historian. He had been most helpful about tracking down sources for footnotes and like matters which hampered her because they were not her style, not because she was not an expert researcher. She wrote Schlesinger that she feared the book lacked "the academic touch" of the other volumes. When she inquired what professional historians had said about the book, he, ever diplomatic, replied vaguely and reassuringly that approval was general, although the usual disagreements over matters "of detail and emphasis" had arisen.[34]

In the 1920's academic historians were generous in acknowledging the contributions of outsiders to their field, and Tarbell's inclusion in *A History of American Life* constitutes such acknowledgment. Reviewers generally ranked the book as one that met the standards of the series, but *The Nation*, of course, demurred. Henry David, *The Nation*'s reviewer, wrote disdainfully, "The volume is smoothly written. Beyond that it has no major virtue, and it is no distinction for the 'A History of American Life' series to have Miss Tarbell's work in it."[35]

CHAPTER 9

An American Conscience

THE annual publication *Paperbound Books in Print* provides an accurate indication of writers' current influence, for only works which appeal to general readers or to teachers, as textbooks for courses, survive the rigorous selection process of public taste. Of Ida Tarbell's many works, two survive in paperback editions: an abridged version of *The History of the Standard Oil Company* and its corollary volume *The Nationalizing of Business, 1878–1898*.[1] Her gentility has become as legendary as the buccaneering activities of the Standard Oil leaders she so successfully assailed. A recent article in *American Heritage,* entitled "The Gentlewoman and the Robber Baron," triangulates the situation with a historian's precision. In the article, the author, Virginia V. Hamilton, focuses on Tarbell's interviews with H. H. Rogers of the Standard Oil Company that were conducted while she was gathering material for her history of the company. Tarbell proved to be a formidable antagonist, and her co-optation by the baronial Rogers which cynics had predicted failed to occur. Instead, Hamilton affirms, Tarbell "presented a remarkably truthful picture of the rise of Standard Oil."[2]

The historic encounter between Ida Tarbell and the forces represented by the Standard Oil Company lives on in the public's memory; but all the other productions of her variegated career are forgotten—biographies which once were best sellers, studies of twentieth-century industry and industrial leaders, explorations of the role of women in industrial society, many uncollected articles, and her autobiography. The reason is that only the issues she raised in *The History of the Standard Oil Company* have continued to be of vital ongoing concern for the nation. The rest is history.

I *Tarbell as a Myth-maker*

Tarbell generated one enduring American myth and ratified two others. The first is the myth of Lincoln's frontier greatness;

the second, that of the business leader selflessly dedicated
to public service; the third, that of his female counterpart,
the housewife, devoting herself to the rearing of young democratic America. It is not surprising that the turbulent 1890's
gave rise to two complementary hypotheses concerning the
role of the frontier in the shaping of American society—that
of Frederick Jackson Turner, who postulated that frontier
experience had impressed itself on the American character
and formed American democracy; and that of Ida Tarbell, that
Lincoln's frontier background was the cause of his greatness
and the salvation of American democracy. While both
hypotheses have been modified by later researchers, neither
has been discarded.

Serious commentators on American society usually have an
inner vision of it which gives direction to their work. Tarbell
had such a vision, and it was gradually articulated in the assignments she received as a writer for *McClure's* and for *The
American*—seemingly random assignments which she wove
together into her version of the perennially elusive American
Dream. Before starting work on her biography of Lincoln, Tarbell had purged herself of lingering notions about the efficacy
of revolution and feminism as vehicles of social progress. She
had begun her research into the activities of Madame Roland
with the expectation that she would find that Madame Roland
had played a moderating, pacific part during the Revolution.
Instead, the Frenchwoman, driven by the demons of "a politician with a Providence complex," had been an early instigator
of the violence which eventually led to her own execution.
A heavier blow had been Tarbell's disillusionment with
revolution itself, for she discovered that revolution, far from
being a "divine weapon" for rooting out evil and replacing
it with justice, was a cyclonic destroyer which had left in its
wake "the same relative proportion of good and evil as it had
started with."[3] This generalization, which resulted from her
study of the French Revolution and its consequences, was
verified by her personal observation of revolutionary activities
from the windows of her Paris apartment in the early 1890's.
The skirmishes she observed between the revolutionary activists and the military forces which quelled them seemed like
stylized memorials of 1789. Likewise, her study of Napoleon
convinced her that the European political system had tragically

misled him into seeking power for himself rather than social reforms for the people.

In Lincoln she found the touchstone for democracy. Then, in her next assignment for *McClure's,* she discovered in Napoleonic John D. Rockefeller a foil for Lincoln, for the magnate's revolutionary business methods represented a threat to the American way of life established by Abraham Lincoln. Rockefeller, she felt, presented an anomaly in the normal evolution of the United States, one caused by unbridled greed and justified by a hypocrisy which spread corruption throughout the nation. To counter the threat, she proposed government regulation rather than the radical solution of Socialism, then very commonly advocated by utopian and Marxist Socialists.

Tarbell's series about the tariff written for *The American Magazine* continued her attack on big businessmen and their political henchmen. *The Tariff in Our Times* was soon followed by the Supreme Court decision dissolving the Standard Oil Company. Never after that did Tarbell attack business; instead, she began to report its positive contributions to the welfare of society. She seized upon use of the Taylor efficiency techniques in industrial concerns as evidence of a cooperative spirit becoming manifest among businessmen that had converted them from "robber barons" to "industrial statesmen." Despite labor's insistence that the Taylor efficiency methods were in reality a subterfuge for production speed-ups and were therefore exploitative of factory workers, Tarbell remained convinced that the Taylor methods, if applied in the spirit of the Golden Rule by both management and labor, could lead to a democratic capitalism in the Lincolnian tradition.

In her biography of Elbert H. Gary she divined in the leader of the United States Steel Corporation an evolutionary force in the progress of business toward social responsibility. And in her biography of Owen D. Young she had found him to be the ideal business leader who not only built a great industry but also devoted many years to distinguished public service. As a writer and reformer, Tarbell had been signally influential in bringing about fundamental reforms in the relationship of business and government. This tremendous achievement quite naturally remained for her a high water mark in the fight for social justice. Nor is it remarkable that her faith in the sanction of government regulation of business should be reinforced by increased awareness among businessmen of their responsibility to the public.

David M. Chalmers notes concerning Tarbell's changed attitude toward business in her later works that "common to all these works was the belief that a sense of social responsibility was spontaneously developing within the American business community."[4] In the midst of the Depression in the 1930's, she continued to rely on the good faith of industrialists as the surest guarantee of justice for their workers. Dismayed by the rise of powerful and militant labor organizations like the Congress of Industrial Organizations, she maintained, concerning Owen D. Young: "I still believe that if we could have had him active in these past years so disheartening for peaceful industrial relations, the years which have set back so far the hope of genuine understanding cooperation within industry, we should have been saved the peck of trouble we are now in."[5]

II Fallacies and Fancies

Tarbell exerted great influence upon American women through communications media, including the radio; for she had long been regarded by the press and public relations people as a sort of semiofficial spokeswoman for her sex. She was highly regarded by other women writers and artists and was for over thirty years president of the Pen and Brush Club, organized by her and other professionals in those fields. But she sincerely believed that most women are the intellectual and emotional inferiors of men. She advised women to remain at home, noting wryly that women's suffrage had not changed politics perceptibly. The average woman would be better off, she thought, learning how to run her household with factory efficiency, leaving conduct of other than local affairs to men. Despite public distrust of politicians, the refusal of organized labor to take seriously her recipe for peaceful industrial relations, and the rejection of her conservative stand on women's rights by militant feminists, there is little doubt that a Gallup poll would confirm that public attitudes concerning the role of Abraham Lincoln in shaping the course of American democracy, those regarding the benevolence of business, or attitudes toward the status of women, remain substantially the same as Ida Tarbell's. A quick survey of Lincoln's Birthday speeches, of corporate publicity, of advertisements aimed at the female consumer will convince most persons of that possibility.

As her reverence for Lincoln deepened, Tarbell seemed to forget the implications of the conversation between him and his younger colleague Ralph Emerson which took place when both were lawyers in Illinois. Lincoln had replied to Emerson's blunt query about the compatibility of the practice of law and of the Golden Rule with a long pause followed by a change of subject. Satisfied that he had an answer, Emerson had quit practice; Lincoln had not done so; and he had soon after returned to the morally ambiguous arena of politics. Few persons can cope with the burdens of darkness, despair, and guilt under which Lincoln often staggered. Tarbell shunned uncertainty and avoided spiritual and emotional depths in her writing; she also disliked introspection, as she admitted in the short-lived journal she started to write after her father died. The Golden Rule seemed to exert upon her an almost tropic attraction; it dazzled her with its apparent attainability. To Lincoln, on the other hand, the ancient axiom must often have seemed as unattainable as a star seen from the bottom of a well.

Yet her temperament aided Tarbell to become a reform-minded journalist; she lived close to the surface of events and thus was encouraged to espouse persuasive, facile solutions for their dislocations: new laws would reform business; a Christian outlook would reform businessmen; labor would best be served by trusting management; women, by trusting everyone—but themselves. The paternalistic society she envisioned under the benevolent alliance of government and business did not allow for competing interest groups. Tarbell's pursuit of harmony led to some debatable conclusions and she seemed at times to confuse paternalism and democracy.

The economist John Kenneth Galbraith recently updated Thorstein Veblen's dictum in *The Theory of the Leisure Class:* " 'According to the ideal scheme of the pecuniary culture, the lady of the house is the head menial of the household." According to Galbraith, Veblen's observation, made in 1899, applies as well to American society almost three-quarters of a century later.[6] Tarbell sentimentally maintained that women's love for their families removed any aura of meniality from their lives, but her easy dismissal of them to an endless round of small tasks and small talk amounts to much the same thing, an acceptance of the idea of women as servants. While Galbraith retains the objectivity proper for an economist, it is clear in his article that he does not accept that idea; he maintains that the economy of the United States is dependent on the exploitation of women's labor in their homes, and he argues that passage of the Equal Rights Amendment is a necessary first step toward their "emancipation." He views marriage in its present state as "a comprehensive trap" for wives. He concedes that "a tolerant society should not think ill of a woman who finds contentment in sexual intercourse, child-bearing, child-rearing, personal adornment, and administration of consumption." He insists, on the other hand, that a tolerant society also "should certainly think ill of a society that offers no alternative—and which ascribes virtue to what is really the convenience of the producers of goods."[7]

Galbraith foresees, not disruption, but a more humane society resulting from a wider choice of life-styles for women. He denies the convention, which was upheld by Tarbell, of frowning on outlets for women that might conflict with "good household management" and observes that a married woman "may serve on a local library board or on a committee to consider delinquency among the young. She may not, without reproach, have full-time employment or a demanding avocation. To do so is to have it said she is neglecting her home and family, that is, her *real* work."[8] Tarbell would have subscribed to Galbraith's statement of the situation but have considered his ironic tone frivolous. In her estimation, motherhood was the great emancipator of women. Tarbell's espousal of a democracy based upon the household drudgery of half the population seems closely analagous to the ancient Greeks' acceptance of an Athenian democracy based on slave labor.

It could appear that Tarbell's underlying aim during the height of her influence as a journalist was to promote the interests of her own group, the white, Anglo-Saxon, Protestant middle class that was fearful of a feudal take-over by the new industrialists on one hand and of ethnic obliteration by immigrant hordes on the other. But such a view of Tarbell's intent is an oversimplification. Instead, her essentially Chautauquan vision was of an industrialized America that retained, while renewing, the institutions of the pre–Civil War era into which she had been born. Never did she advocate the imposition of these institutions or the values which helped create them, for it never seriously occurred to her to question that they were the culmination of Western civilization—Eastern civilization had only colonial status in those days, and an African one was thought to be nonexistent. The vision implicit in Tarbell's work was compounded of nostalgia for the past and a plan for a future that was to be organically evolved from it; and the vision revealed her belief in a human nature sufficiently perfectible to base actions as well as prayers on the Golden Rule. Thus would come into being a social order that would be assuredly the product of much sweat, but of no blood and few tears.

It is not difficult to understand the appeal for her and thousands like her of Mussolini's Italy of the 1920's, for he too beckoned the future from the past. In Tarbell's words, he found in Fascism "the genius of a race reborn, the Latin tradition always at work... the return of the Roman idea of the State and to the faith of Christ. It is the union of the great past to a luminous future. Fascism is the cult of spiritual values as opposed to the cult of the belly, which is the only god which Socialists, Anarchists, and Communists recognize. Fascism is the liberty of the Italian people, replacing the frightful license of individuals, groups, parties; it is the triumph of work, order, discipline."[9]

Similarly, Tarbell yearned for a future formed from the democratic past. That her projected paradise would inevitably be ethnocentric and elitist she would sincerely have denied because of her zeal for this best of all possible worlds. Such zeal, however, easily becomes subject to abstraction, loses sight of individuals, and manipulates groups into positions which please the planner, and thus becomes fatally solipsistic. Tarbell's ideal society, however real it seemed to her, is reminiscent of the toylike model communities erected by architects and urban planners. The multicultural pressures of the ethnically pluralistic American society which have become evident in recent times were at work even as she formulated her vision which was tidily contained behind a white picket fence straight out of early nineteenth-century New England.

Like all great propagandists, Tarbell prepared the ground in *The History of the Standard Oil Company* before planting seeds which could flower into reform legislation; for she was aware that there has to be some correlation between law and custom. Perhaps her great miscalculation at the height of her career was her too optimistic assumption that such a correlation was present between the Golden Rule and custom. Later, when she no longer echoed as a journalist the desires and aspirations of middle America and when she had become in the 1930's a reminder of the American past, her philosophy had become less sentimental, more stoic, more austerely pragmatic: "The time, the place, the need, the relation are what determine the value of an act."[10] To embody nobly and without bitterness such a creed was Ida Tarbell's final achievement. But her earlier optimism, tempered in a disordered world she had never anticipated, sustained to the end her faith in the ultimate rationality of mankind as a source of order and her conviction that "work ... backed up by such a faith makes life endurable."[11]

III *Ida Tarbell's Legacy*

Few journalists or historians have made history; journalists report daily events and historians interpret them. But Tarbell joins the select company of propagandists like Thomas Paine and Harriet Beecher Stowe whose works were like bugle calls to battle. Paine's *Common Sense* and the American Revolution are inseparable; Abraham Lincoln referred to Stowe only half-facetiously as the little lady whose book, *Uncle Tom's Cabin*, caused the Civil War; Tarbell is remembered as the journalist who bested the robber barons in a fair fight and scotched the reptilian principle of special privilege that they had attempted to substitute for the historic American principle of equal opportunity. All three writers unlocked the reservoirs of moral energy needed in times of grave national crisis when national identity was at stake and with it, seemingly, survival.

Tarbell cannot be termed a great writer, for too little of her work has endured. Her equipment as a writer was modest, but she used it well. She often achieved the sort of lucidity in her prose which paradoxically conceals beneath its very transparency the intelligence and the workmanship that make it possible. She had no aptitude for fiction, as her one novel, *The Rising of the Tide*, clearly demonstrates. She possessed a flair for illumination of character through anecdotes which enlivened her works. She also possessed steadiness, integrity, and moral courage, and it was these qualities rather than technical brilliance which lent distinction to her writing. Only in *The History of the Standard Oil Company* did intense moral outrage succeed in lifting her style from pedestrian competence to inspired lightning-bolt paragraphs and cliff-hanger chapter endings. Her main contributions as a writer were those of a pioneer, for she carried out the pioneer spirit of her ancestors in all her undertakings. She was among the first of the emancipated New Women to attend college, and she subsequently became among the foremost of the new journalists who are remembered as Muckrakers. In addition, she was a seminal pioneer in the writing of business history and in Lincoln studies. The body of her work stands as a memorial to a great journalist who initiated a tradition of responsible journalism which has continued to serve the nation well during succeeding times of national crisis.

The History of the Standard Oil Company is a particularly relevant cautionary tale at the present time, when the relationship of business and government seems once again to many observers to be working against the public interest. The morality which underlies Tarbell's historic work seems today somewhat old-fashioned in its expression and naïve in its expectations. But perhaps it is not overoptimistic to state that the same moral idealism is operational in the United States of the 1970's; were this not so, Tarbell's great work would be forgotten entirely. Instead, since her death in 1944, she has remained in the national awareness as a subliminal conscience warning Americans against their cardinal sin of materialism. Her one great work, *The History of the Standard Oil Company*, remains a timeless philippic that denounces the American Sin. She posed in it a question not yet resolved: Can democracy and corporate capitalism coexist?

Notes and References

Chapter One

1. *All in the Day's Work* (New York, 1939), p. 9.
2. *Ibid.*, p. 10. A fourth child, Franklin Sumner Tarbell, Jr., had died of scarlet fever.
3. *Ibid.*
4. *Ibid.*, p. 16.
5. *Ibid.*
6. *Ibid.*, p. 21.
7. *Ibid.*, p. 44.
8. *Ibid.*, p. 26.
9. *Ibid.*, p. 51.
10. "The Arts and Industries of Cincinnati," *The Chautauquan*, VII (December, 1886), 162.
11. *Ibid.*
12. *All in the Day's Work*, p. 87.
13. *Ibid.*, pp. 55–56.

Chapter Two

1. Ida M. Tarbell Papers, Sophia Smith Collection, Smith College Library, Northampton, Massachusetts. Newspaper clipping, no title, n.d.
2. "Women in Journalism," *The Chautauquan*, VII (April, 1887), 393.
3. *Madame Roland: A Biographical Study* (New York, 1896), p. ix.
4. *Madame Roland*, p. 224.
5. Tarbell remained firmly convinced that it is a "natural law" that a woman's prime purpose is to "back up her man," right or wrong (*All in the Day's Work*, p. 143).
6. *Madame Roland*, pp. 288–89.
7. Paul De Roux, ed., *Mémoires de Madame Roland* (Paris, 1966), p. 216 ff.
8. *All in the Day's Work*, p. 153.
9. *Ibid.*, p. 151.
10. Samuel Sidney McClure, *My Autobiography* (New York, 1914), p. 220. McClure, a brilliant editor but no writer, had Willa Cather, then an editor of *McClure's*, ghostwrite his "autobiography." The book is McClure; Willa Cather managed to give the impression of

merely editing his conversation. McClure's joy at besting the *Century* comes through "loud, clear, and undiluted."

11. McClure thought most experts were poor writers because their style was dull, overdetailed, and turgid. Instead, he developed generalists who could turn their talents to a study in depth of a subject within their competence.

12. *A Life of Napoleon Bonaparte* (New York, 1905), p. 451.

13. *Ibid.*, p. 452.

14. *All in the Day's Work*, p. 152. Tarbell did not take the Napoleon biography very seriously, seemingly partly because the text played second fiddle to the illustrations.

15. *Napoleon*, pp. 129–32.

16. *Ibid.*, p. 294.

Chapter Three

1. Benjamin P. Thomas, *Portrait for Posterity* (New Brunswick, N.J., 1947), pp. 112 ff. The Abraham Lincoln papers did not become available to scholars until 1947, and their release opened an entirely new era in Lincoln studies.

2. Peter Lyon, *Success Story* (New York, 1963), pp. 137–38.

3. Tarbell, *The Life of Abraham Lincoln* (New York, 1900), v. I, p. viii.

4. *All in the Day's Work*, p. 163.

5. *Ibid.*

6. John Coleman Adams, "Lincoln's Place in History," *Century Magazine*, XLVII (February, 1894), 590, 594.

7. Carl Schurz, *Abraham Lincoln: An Essay* (Boston, 1891), p. 1. Revised and reprinted from an essay in *The Atlantic Monthly*, June, 1891.

8. *Ibid.*, p. 3.

9. *All in the Day's Work*, pp. 169, 170.

10. *The Life of Abraham Lincoln*, I, p. 265.

11. James Fenimore Cooper, *The Prairie* (New York, 1859), p. 68.

12. Herbert Hoover once told Ida Tarbell that he had read her biography of Lincoln because he had stayed during World War I at a hotel in Rotterdam which owned only two books in English, her Lincoln biography and Edward Gibbon's *History of the Decline and Fall of the Roman Empire.* Tarbell graciously agreed with Hoover's criticism, saying she would have given ten years of her life to have experienced the Civil War. Her only memory was of her parents' grief when Lincoln was assassinated and of doors in Rouseville that were decked in black in mourning after his death.

13. Review of *The Life of Abraham Lincoln*, *The Nation*, LXX (March 1, 1900), 164.

14. *The Life of Abraham Lincoln*, II, p. 262.

15. Benjamin P. Thomas, "Our Lincoln Heritage from Ida Tarbell," *Abraham Lincoln Quarterly*, VI (March, 1950), 21.

16. Thomas, *Portrait for Posterity*, p. 192 ff.

17. *Ibid.*

18. *Ibid.*, p. 201.

19. Tarbell's experience in Civil War research is impressive. In addition to works appearing under her own name, she served as ghostwriter for Charles A. Dana's *Recollection of the Civil War*, which ran in *McClure's* in 1897 and 1898. Dana, then the editor of the New York *Sun*, had served in the Lincoln administration as assistant secretary of war. Following the Dana assignment, Tarbell was made editorial assistant to Carl Schurz while he wrote his reminiscences for *McClure's*.

20. Isabel Paterson, review of *In the Footsteps of the Lincolns*, New York *Tribune*, February 17, 1924.

21. McClure, *My Autobiography*, p. 238.

Chapter Four

1. *The History of the Standard Oil Company* (Gloucester, Mass., 1963), I, pp. 3–4.

2. *Ibid.*, I, p. ix.

3. There are minor rearrangements in the sequence of chapters in the book, but the unrevised text of the *McClure's* articles was retained, with the addition of the appendix.

4. Editorial, *McClure's Magazine*, November, 1903, 111.

5. Refunds were partial repayments to a company for its own shipments. Drawbacks were refunds to a company on rival shipments.

6. Allan Nevins, *Study in Power: John D. Rockefeller* (New York, 1953), I. pp. 1–5.

7. *Ibid.*, p. 9.

8. *Ibid.*, II, p. 228. Nevins notes that by 1890 there were "fully fifty trusts." Lloyd listed four hundred in *Wealth Against Commonwealth*.

9. McClure, *My Autobiography*, pp. 265–66.

10. *All in the Day's Work*, p. 240.

11. *The History of the Standard Oil Company*, I, pp. 36–37.

12. Gilbert Holland Montague, *The Rise and Progress of the Standard Oil Company* (New York, 1903), pp. 22–23.

13. *Ibid.*, p. 24.

14. *Ibid.*, pp. 28, 33.

15. *Ibid.*, pp. 33–34.

16. Nevins, *Study in Power*, I, p. 131.

17. Henry Demarest Lloyd, *Wealth Against Commonwealth*, ed. Thomas C. Cochran (Englewood Cliffs, N.J., 1963), p. 30. Except

where otherwise noted, quotations from Lloyd's work are taken from Cochran's edition.

18. *The History of the Standard Oil Company*, II, pp. 256–57.
19. Montague, *The Rise and Progress of the Standard Oil Company*, p. 18; Nevins, *Study in Power*, I, p. 130.
20. *The History of the Standard Oil Company*, I, p. 101.
21. *Ibid.*, p. 207.
22. *Ibid.*
23. *Ibid.*, p. 204.
24. *Ibid.*, pp. 203–05.
25. *Ibid.*, p. 206.
26. *Ibid.*, pp. 205–06.
27. Gilbert Holland Montague, "The Legend of the Standard Oil Company," *North American Review*, CLXXX (September, 1905), 362–63.
28. Nevins, *Study in Power*, II, p. 138.
29. John D. Rockefeller, "Random Reminiscences of Men and Events," *The Master Workers' Book* (Garden City, N.Y., 1916), p. 107.
30. *Ibid.*, p. 111.
31. *Ibid.*, p. 112.
32. *The History of the Standard Oil Company*, II, p. 12.
33. *Ibid.*, pp. 3–30.
34. Nevins, *Study in Power*, I, p. 380.

Chapter Five

1. *The History of the Standard Oil Company*, II, p. 66.
2. *Ibid.*, I, document number 48 in appendix, "Report of the Special Master Commissioner George K. Nash to the Circuit Court," pp. 348–54. Text of the commissioner's report concerning the Rice case to the Circuit Court of the United States, Southern District of Ohio, Eastern Division.
3. *The History of the Standard Oil Company*, II, 85–86.
4. Montague, *The Rise and Progress of the Standard Oil Company*, pp. 97–98.
5. Nevins, *Study in Power,* II, p. 77.
6. *The History of the Standard Oil Company*, II, p. 88.
7. Henry Demarest Lloyd, *Wealth Against Commonwealth*, (New York, 1894), pp. 263–64.
8. *The History of the Standard Oil Company*, II, pp. 88–109.
9. *Ibid.*, p. 110.
10. *Ibid.*
11. Montague, "The Legend of the Standard Oil Company," p. 362.
12. *Ibid.*
13. Nevins, *Study in Power*, II, p. 78.
14. *The History of the Standard Oil Company*, II, pp. 117–18.

15. *Ibid.*, p. 119.

16. Montague, "The Legend of the Standard Oil Company," p. 362.

17. Nevins, *Study in Power*, II, p. 334.

18. Montague, *The Rise and Progress of the Standard Oil Company*, p. 143.

19. Nevins, *Study in Power*, II, p. 384.

20. *Ibid.*, p. 385.

21. *All in the Day's Work*, p. 240.

22. Ida Tarbell was thus advertised in *The American Magazine*, May, 1915.

23. Ida M. Tarbell, "John D. Rockefeller: A Character Study," *McClure's Magazine*, XXV (July, 1905), 227.

24. *Ibid.*, p. 243.

25. *The History of the Standard Oil Company*, II, p. 288.

26. Tarbell papers, Allegheny College Library, Meadville, Pennsylvania., n.p., May 25, 1922. Letter to the historian C. C. Regier, then writing at the University of Iowa his dissertation which involved the Muckrakers.

27. *All in the Day's Work*, p. 250.

28. *Ibid.*

29. *Ibid.*, p. 204.

30. Tarbell papers, Allegheny College Library. The quotation appeared in a column entitled "Book Talk," by John S. Phillips, in a weekly paper, *The Independent Republican*, May 9, 1939. The clipping found in the Tarbell papers did not specify Goshen, New York, as the place of publication, but it almost certainly is, since Phillips was a resident of Goshen at the time and since no other publication of that time bears the same title.

Chapter Six

1. "Court of Hope and Goodwill," *The American Magazine*, LXXVII (January, 1914), 43.

2. Tarbell papers, Allegheny College Library. Journal entry dated May 5, 1905.

3. Tarbell's journal contains an interesting account of her encounter with Henry James, who remained Olympian to her despite her reportorial observation the next day that he had a bit of breakfast egg on his face.

4. *All in the Day's Work*, p. 45.

5. Caroline T. Trambell, "Ida M. Tarbell and Her Farm," *Country Life in America*, XXIX (November, 1915), 22.

6. The article appeared in *McClure's Magazine*, in the March, 1906, issue.

7. *All in the Day's Work*, p. 256.

8. *Ibid.*, pp. 258–59.

9. *Ibid.*, p. 268.

10. "Where Every Penny Counts," *The American Magazine*, LXVII (March, 1909), 449.

11. "Mr. Aldrich and the Tariff: His Ideas and Methods of Revision as Seen in the Making of the Cotton Schedule of 1909—The True Citadel of Protection," *The American Magazine*, LXXI (December, 1910), 222.

12. "The Stand-Pat Intellect," *The American Magazine*, LXXII (May, 1911), 41.

13. "Testing the Tariff by Its Moral Effects," *The American Magazine*, LXXII (June, 1911), 186.

14. "Words From Women," Sunday feature in Lansing, Michigan, *State Journal*, CXVI, July 19, 1970.

15. "The Business of Being a Woman," *The American Magazine*, LXXIII (March, 1912), 563.

16. Tarbell papers, Sophia Smith Collection, Smith College Library. Letter to John S. Phillips, n.p., n.d. (*circa* 1912).

17. *Ibid.*

18. *All in the Day's Work*, p. 280.

19. "The Gospel of Safety," third article of series *The Golden Rule in Business*, *The American Magazine*, LXXIX (January, 1915), 30.

20. "His Own Worst Enemy," seventh article of series *The Golden Rule in Business*, *The American Magazine*, LXXIX (May, 1915), 20–23.

21. *Ibid.*

22. *All in the Day's Work*, p. 296.

Chapter Seven

1. "Tattler," *The Nation*, CIV (January 18, 1917), 84.

2. *Ibid.*

3. *All in the Day's Work*, pp. 278–79.

4. "A Talk With the President of the United States," *Collier's Weekly*, LVIII (October 28, 1916), 1.

5. *Ibid.*, p. 41.

6. *All in the Day's Work*, pp. 307–08.

7. Henry Adams, *The United States in 1800*, first six chapters of *History of the United States during the First Administration of Thomas Jefferson* (Ithaca, New York, 1957), pp. 124–25.

8. Tarbell papers, Allegheny College Library. Note on the flyleaf of Tarbell's personal copy of *The Rising of the Tide*, dated January 15, 1930.

9. Tarbell *et al.*, "War! What the Women of America Can Do to Prevent It," *Woman's Day*, April, 1939, 47.

10. *All in the Day's Work*, p. 344.

11. *Ibid.*, 347.

12. *Ibid.*, pp. 357–58.

13. *Peacemakers—Blessed and Otherwise: Observations, Reflections and Irritations at an International Conference* (New York, 1922), pp. 226–27.

14. *All in the Day's Work*, pp. 377–84. The Mussolini pieces were not collected. The series, entitled "The Greatest Story in the World Today," ran in *McCall's Magazine* from November, 1926, through February, 1927. Tarbell's report was almost entirely favorable. She ducked the implications for democracy of Fascism, merely noting hastily in passing that "intelligent liberals" in Italy were opposed to Mussolini's regime because it was antidemocratic. Their opposition is not otherwise discussed. Rather than evaluate further implications, Tarbell dwelt heavily in her concluding article on Mussolini's momentarily expected assassination, and the expected consequent fall of his one-man rule.

15. Tarbell papers, Allegheny College Library. Letter to Olivia Rossetti Agresti, n.p., July 7, 1932.

16. *Ibid.*, letter to S. S. McClure, n.p., December 28, 1921. E. Phillips Oppenheim was a British writer of novels of international intrigue.

Chapter Eight

1. *All in the Day's Work*, pp. 369–70.

2. *The Life of Elbert H. Gary: The Story of Steel* (New York, 1925), p. vi.

3. *Ibid.*, p. 52.

4. *Ibid.*, pp. 123–24.

5. *Ibid.*, p. 124.

6. *Ibid.*, p. 162.

7. *Ibid.*, pp. 165–66.

8. *Ibid.*, pp. 189–90.

9. *Ibid.*, p. 221.

10. *Ibid.*, p. 229.

11. *Ibid.*, p. 319.

12. *Ibid.*, p. 351.

13. *All in the Day's Work*, p. 371.

14. Allan Nevins, review in New York *World*, November 25, 1925. The twelve-hour day was not eliminated in the steel industry until after World War I.

15. Unsigned review in New York *World*, September 3, 1925.

16. Benjamin Stolberg, "St. Elbert of the Heavenly Trust," *The Nation*, CXXII (April 14, 1926), 414–16.

17. Tarbell papers, Allegheny College Library. Course prospectus and student comments on course offered April-May, 1939, at Allegheny College by Ida Tarbell.

18. Esther Hamilton, interview with Ida M. Tarbell carried in Youngstown, Ohio, *Vindicator*, April 30, 1939.

19. Tarbell papers, Sophia Smith Collection, Smith College Library. Outline of old-age study; sketch of projected utopian fantasy.
20. Tarbell papers, Allegheny College Library. Correspondence between Tarbell and George A. Kahn, treasurer of the Bellamy Association, in 1933 and 1934.
21. "New Dealers of the 'Seventies: Henry George and Edward Bellamy," *The Forum*, XCII (September, 1934), 133.
22. *Owen D. Young: A New Type of Industrial Leader* (New York, 1932), p. x.
23. "Why Smith Gets My Vote," *Collier's Weekly*, LXXXII (September 15, 1928), 9.
24. *Ibid*. Harry Sinclair was one of the oil men involved in the Teapot Dome scandal concerning oil leases of government lands during the Warren G. Harding administration.
25. *Ibid*., p. 48.
26. Tarbell papers, Allegheny College Library. Letter, n.p., May 20, 1932, to George Creel.
27. *Ibid*., Tarbell's commentary on a column in the New York *Herald Tribune*, June 6, 1935.
28. *Ibid*., Tarbell's commentary on a Lippmann column in the same newspaper, of April 4, 1935.
29. *Ibid*., correspondence between Arthur M. Schlesinger and Ida M. Tarbell, from the spring of 1923 to the spring of 1936.
30. *The Nationalizing of Business, 1878–1898* (New York, 1936), p. xiii.
31. *Ibid*., pp. xv–xvi.
32. *Ibid*., p. 1.
33. *Ibid*., p. 227
34. See note 29.
35. Henry David, review of *The Nationalizing of Business, 1878–1898*, *The Nation* CXLIII (December 5, 1936), 668.

Chapter Nine

1. The entire *History of American Life* series, of which *The Nationalizing of Business, 1878–1898* is volume nine, has recently been reissued in a paperback edition by Franklin Watts, Inc., New York.
2. Virginia V. Hamilton, "The Gentlewoman and the Robber Baron," *American Heritage*, XXI (April, 1970), 86.
3. *All in the Day's Work*, pp. 143–44.
4. David M. Chalmers, "Ida M. Tarbell," *Notable American Women, 1607–1950* (Cambridge, Mass., 1971).
5. *All in the Day's Work*, p. 388.
6. John Kenneth Galbraith, "The Economics of the American Housewife," *The Atlantic Monthly*, CCXXXII (August, 1973), 79.

7. *Ibid.*, p. 81.

8. *Ibid.*, p. 79.

9. "The Greatest Story in the World Today," *McCall's Magazine* (December, 1926), 83.

10. *All in the Day's Work*, p. 405.

11. *Ibid.*

Selected Bibliography

PRIMARY SOURCES

1. Books

A Short Life of Napoleon Bonaparte. New York: S. S. McClure, 1895.
The Early Life of Abraham Lincoln. With J. McCan Davis. New York: S. S. McClure, 1896.
Madame Roland: A Biographical Study. New York: Scribner's, 1896.
The Life of Abraham Lincoln. 2 vols. New York: McClure, Phillips, 1900.
Napoleon's Addresses. New York: Page, 1902.
History of the Standard Oil Company. 2 vols. New York: S. S. McClure, 1904. Reissued in a one-volume edition including both volumes of the original edition. Gloucester, Massachusetts: Peter Smith, 1963.
A Souvenir of Lincoln's Birthday, February 12, 1907. With F. T. Hill and R. L. Jones. New York: Lincoln Farm Association, 1907.
He Knew Lincoln. New York: S. S. McClure, 1907.
Father Abraham. New York: Moffat, Yard, 1909.
Selections from the Letters, Speeches, and State Papers of Abraham Lincoln. Ed. with an introduction and notes. Boston: Ginn, 1911.
The Tariff in Our Times. New York: Macmillan, 1911.
The Business of Being a Woman. New York: Macmillan, 1912.
Ways of Woman. New York: Macmillan, 1915.
New Ideals in Business: An Account of Their Practice and Their Effects Upon Men and Profits. New York: Macmillan, 1916.
The Rising of the Tide: The Story of Sabinsport. New York: Macmillan, 1919.
In Lincoln's Chair. New York: Macmillan, 1920.
Boy Scout's Life of Lincoln. New York: Macmillan, 1922.
He Knew Lincoln, and Other Billy Brown Stories. New York: Macmillan, 1922.
Peacemakers—Blessed and Otherwise: Observations, Reflections and Irritations at an International Conference. New York: Macmillan, 1922.
In the Footsteps of the Lincolns. New York and London: Harper, 1924.
Life of Elbert H. Gary: The Story of Steel. New York: Appleton, 1925.
A Reporter for Lincoln: Story of Henry E. Wing, Soldier and Newspaper man. New York: Macmillan, 1927.

Owen D. Young: A New Type of Industrial Leader. New York: Macmillan, 1932.

The Nationalizing of Business, 1878–1898. A History of American Life series, ed. A. M. Schlesinger and D. R. Fox, vol. 9. New York: Macmillan, 1936.

Women at Work: A Tour Among Careers. Ed. A. W. Robinson. New York: Career Tours Committee, 1939.

All in the Day's Work: An Autobiography. New York: Macmillan, 1939.

2. Articles

Since the list of Ida Tarbell's articles is long and since a bibliography of her works is available from the Reis Library at Allegheny College, I cite only articles referred to in the text.

"The Arts and Industries of Cincinnati." *The Chautauquan,* VII (December, 1886), 160–62.

"John D. Rockefeller: A Character Study." *McClure's Magazine,* XXV (July, August, 1905), 227–49, 386–98.

"Where Every Penny Counts." *The American Magazine,* LXVII (March, 1909), 437–49. Part of a series published as *The Tariff in Our Times.*

"Mr. Aldrich and the Tariff." *The American Magazine,* LXXI (December), 1910), 212–22. Published in *The Tariff in Our Times.*

"The Stand-Pat Intellect." *The American Magazine,* LXXII (May, 1911), 33–41. Published in *The Tariff in Our Times.*

"Testing the Tariff by Its Moral Effects." *The American Magazine,* LXXII (June, 1911), 183–93. Published in *The Tariff in Our Times.*

"The Business of Being a Woman." *The American Magazine,* LXXIII (March, 1912), 563–68. Title piece of book.

"Court of Hope and Good Will." *The American Magazine,* LXXVII (January, 1914), 42–48.

"The Gospel of Safety." *The American Magazine,* LXXIX (January, 1915), 29–34. Included in *New Ideals in Business.*

"His Own Worst Enemy." *The American Magazine,* LXXIX (May, 1915), 20–23. Included in *New Ideals in Business.*

"A Talk With the President of the United States." *Collier's Weekly,* LVIII (October 28, 1916), 5–6.

"The Greatest Story in the World Today." Series in *McCall's Magazine,* November-December, 1926, January-February, 1927. About Mussolini.

"Why Smith Gets My Vote." *Collier's Weekly,* LXXXII (September 15, 1928), 8–9.

"New Dealers of the 'Seventies: Henry George and Edward Bellamy." *The Forum*, XCII (September, 1934), 133–39.

"War! What the Women of America Can Do to Prevent It." *Woman's Day*, April, 1939. Tarbell and other notable women interviewed.

3. Papers

The most extensive collection of Tarbell's papers is in the Reis Library of Allegheny College, Meadville, Pennsylvania. Documents concerning her entire career are held there, as well as her extensive Lincoln Library and other related material. The Drake Memorial Museum in nearby Titusville, Pennsylvania, has documents relating primarily to Tarbell's research for *The History of the Standard Oil Company*; others are concerned with her later work on Standard Oil, including the abortive series for McClure's in the 1920's. Unless the papers have recently been put into some order, they are not very useful for systematic investigation. The documents in the Sophia Smith Collection at Smith College, Northampton, Massachusetts, which are well arranged, are limited mostly to early Lincoln research materials.

SECONDARY SOURCES

1. Autobiographies by Tarbell Colleagues
The following accounts by Tarbell's colleagues generally verify and add dimension to her own account of her times. In addition, the writers listed are unanimous in their admiration of Ida Tarbell and her work.

BAKER, RAY STANNARD. *Native American*. New York: Scribner's, 1941. Covers the years of Baker's youth as a typical Midwestern boy.
———. *An American Chronicle*. New York: Scribner's, 1945. Continues Baker's recollections from 1892 and is characterized by his intelligent grasp of events during the muckraking era.
McCLURE, SAMUEL SIDNEY. *My Autobiography*. New York: Stokes, 1914. Ghostwritten by Willa Cather, then an associate editor of *McClure's*. Captures the verve and egotism of its subject and provides information about the working relationship between McClure and his staff.
STEFFENS, LINCOLN. *The Autobiography of Lincoln Steffens*. New York: Harcourt, 1931. Steffens's wide contacts furnish graphic cameos of movers and shakers. Provides rationale for the Socialism Steffens embraced in later years.
WHITE, WILLIAM ALLEN. *The Autobiography of William Allen White*. New York: Macmillan, 1946. Another Midwestern boyhood

account which describes the spirit of a small Kansas community. Provides insight into economic forces of the early twentieth century.

2. General Sources

ADAMS, HENRY. *The Education of Henry Adams.* Boston: Houghton Mifflin, 1930. Classic account of the post–Civil War era told from an attitude of disenchantment.
———. *The United States in 1800.* Ithaca, N.Y.: Cornell University Press, 1957. Consists of the first six chapters of Volume I of Henry Adams's *History of the United States of America during the First Administration of Thomas Jefferson,* published by Scribner's in 1889. Brilliant overview of American culture at the turn of the century.

BANNISTER, ROBERT. *Ray Stannard Baker, the Mind and Thought of a Progressive.* New Haven, Conn.: Yale University Press, 1966. Sympathetic revaluation of the Progressive era and of Baker's role then and later in American affairs, particularly his association with Woodrow Wilson.

CHAMBERLAIN, JOHN. *Farewell to Reform.* New York: Liveright, 1932. Attacks the Progressive movement as superficial in its approach to social reform. Dismisses Ida Tarbell as a serious reformer because she allegedly "sold out" to write in favor of big business following the end of muckraking.

COCHRAN, THOMAS C., and WILLIAM MILLER. *The Age of Enterprise.* New York: Harper, 1961. Second, revised edition of an earlier (1942) study; a well-written social history of American industrialism up to World War II.

COOPER, JAMES FENIMORE. *The Prairie.* New York: Rinehart, 1859. Discerning examination of the frontier and tensions among trapper-explorers, Indians, and settlers in the early nineteenth century. Aids understanding of the frontier environment of Abraham Lincoln and also that of Ida Tarbell.

FILLER, LOUIS. *Crusaders for American Liberalism: The Story of the Muckrakers.* New York: Crowell-Collier, 1961. Reprint of the 1939 edition; full, interesting study of the period. Tempers harsh criticism of the Muckrakers by earlier writers of the 1930's.

FLEMING, ALICE. *Ida Tarbell: First of the Muckrakers.* New York: Thomas Y. Crowell Company, 1971. One of the *Women of America* series (Milton Meltzer, ed.) written for juvenile readers. A swift-moving account of Tarbell's career with emphasis on her study of the Standard Oil Company.

FLYNN, JOHN T. *God's Gold: The Study of John D. Rockefeller and His Times.* New York: Harcourt Brace, 1932. Interesting study; emphasizes the role of propaganda in both the early image of

Rockefeller as a corporate villain, created by Tarbell, and the later one as philanthropic benefactor, devised by press agents.
———. *Men of Wealth.* New York: Simon and Schuster, 1941. Short accounts of wealthy men beginning with the fifteenth-century financier Jacob Fugger; includes J. D. Rockefeller as "the builder" representative of his times.

LLOYD, HENRY DEMAREST. *Wealth Against Commonwealth.* New York: Harper, 1894. Original edition of Lloyd's scathing attack on the unnamed John D. Rockefeller and his oil trust.
———. *Wealth Against Commonwealth.* Thomas C. Cochran, ed. Englewood Cliffs, N.J.: Prentice-Hall, 1963. Abridged version; omits parts of the original that the editor found unreliable.
———. *Lords of Industry.* New York: Putnam, 1910. Posthumous collection of articles; includes the first attack on Standard Oil, Lloyd's "The Story of a Great Monopoly," published in *The Atlantic Monthly* (March, 1881).

LYON, PETER. *Success Story.* New York: Scribner's, 1963. Beautifully written biography of S. S. McClure; sympathetically but objectively evaluates his role as a journalistic innovator.

MONTAGUE, GILBERT HOLLAND. *The Rise and Progress of the Standard Oil Company.* New York: Harper, 1903. This academic (Harvard University) monograph is widely believed to have been subsidized as a publication by the Standard Oil Company to counter the devastating effects of Tarbell's series on the company, concurrently appearing in *McClure's Magazine.*

MORRIS, LLOYD. *Postscript to Yesterday.* New York: Random House, 1947. Brilliantly traces the change in Americans' outlook from the optimism of pre–World War I to the confusion and doubt following World War II.

MOTT, FRANK LUTHER. *A History of American Magazines, 1885–1905,* vol. 4. Cambridge, Mass.: Harvard University Press, 1957. Invaluable source of information about the rise of modern magazines; good studies of McClure and Tarbell as leading figures in rise of mass-circulation periodicals.

NEVINS, ALLAN. *John D. Rockefeller: The Heroic Age of American Enterprise.* 2 vols. New York: Scribner's, 1940. This study of Rockefeller and Standard Oil complements Tarbell's by emphasizing the company's side of the controversy. Nevins retains objectivity while defending Rockefeller.
———. *Study in Power: John D. Rockefeller.* 2 vols. New York: Scribner's, 1953. A revised edition of the earlier book on Rockefeller; new material added but retains same viewpoint.

PETERSON, THEODORE. *Magazines in the Twentieth Century.* Urbana: University of Illinois Press, 1956. Supplements Mott's *History of American Magazines.*

RICHMOND, REBECCA. *Chautauqua; An American Place.* New York: Duell, Sloan, 1943. Informative history of the Chautauqua movement.

ROCKEFELLER, JOHN D. "Random Reminiscences of Men and Events," in *The Master Worker's Book.* Garden City, N.Y.: Doubleday, 1916. Reprint of original 1909 edition. Rockefeller's defense of his record. Presents the impression of a wary, drily witty man whose esthetic ideal was efficiency.

DE ROUX, PAUL, ed. *Mémoires de Madame Roland.* Paris: Mercure de France, 1966. The French Revolutionary heroine's romantic, yet forthright and unflinching, view of high points in her life provides insight into her personality not available in Tarbell's biography, for each writer had a differing perception of the protagonist.

SCHLESINGER, ARTHUR M. *The Rise of the City, 1878–1898. A History of American Life* series, ed. A. M. Schlesinger and D. R. Fox, vol. 10. New York: Macmillan, 1933. Companion volume to Tarbell's *The Nationalizing of Business, 1878–1898.* Details cultural events paralleling the economic events covered in her economic overview of the period.

SCHURZ, CARL. *Abraham Lincoln: An Essay.* Boston: Houghton Mifflin, 1891. Calls for fresh viewpoints about Lincoln.

THOMAS, BENJAMIN P. *Portrait for Posterity.* New Brunswick, N.J.: Rutgers University Press, 1947. Definitive evaluation of Lincoln biographers up to early 1940's. Rates Tarbell as transitional figure between early Romantic and modern Realistic biographers of Lincoln.

3. Articles and Reviews

ADAMS, JOHN COLEMAN. "Lincoln's Place in History." *Century Magazine,* XLVII (February, 1894), 590–96. Lincoln's "place" is that of savior of the Union.

ANONYMOUS. Review of Tarbell's *Life of Abraham Lincoln. The Nation,* LXX (March 1, 1900), 164. Favorable but condescending view of the book as a popularization.

———. Review of Tarbell's *The History of the Standard Oil Company. The Nation,* LXXX (January 5, 1905), 15–16. Critical of Tarbell's bias against the Standard Oil Company as a seriously distorting element in her analysis.

———. Review of Tarbell's *Life of Elbert H. Gary,* New York *World,* September 3, 1925. Expresses disappointment over Tarbell's apparent switch to a pro-business bias.

CHALMERS, DAVID M. "From Robber Barons to Industrial Statesmen: Standard Oil and the Business Historian." *American Journal of Economics and Sociology,* XX (October, 1960), 47–58. Condemns materialism of business historians of the 1950's. Extols idealism and values of earlier historians, particularly those of Tarbell's history of Standard Oil, as conducive to meaningful evaluation rather than complacent acceptance of materialistic business values.

————. "Ida M. Tarbell." *Notable American Women, 1607–1950.* Cambridge, Mass.: Harvard University Press, 1971. Short biography and sympathetic evaluation of Tarbell's work.

DAVID, HENRY. Review of *The Nationalizing of Business, 1878–1898. The Nation*, CXLIII (December 5, 1936), 666, 668. The reviewer is critical of Tarbell's scholarship and her lack of objectivity, and notes her fondness for the "strong men" of the period. David consistently upholds *The Nation's* denigration of Tarbell.

DESTLER, CHESTER MCA. "Wealth Against Commonwealth." *American Historical Review*, L (October, 1944), 49–69. Defends H. D. Lloyd against charges by Allan Nevins of dishonest reporting.

HAMILTON, ESTHER. Interview with Ida M. Tarbell. Youngstown, Ohio *Vindicator*, April 30, 1939. Stresses Tarbell's marked vitality.

HAMILTON, VIRGINIA V. "The Gentlewoman and the Robber Baron." *American Heritage*, XXI (April, 1970), 78–86. Comments upon the David vs. Goliath aspect of Tarbell's investigation of Standard Oil. Notes Tarbell's weakness in economics, her moral bias, and her comparatively inadequate research tools as flaws in what remains a truthful and valid investigation.

MONTAGUE, GILBERT HOLLAND. "The Legend of the Standard Oil Company." *North American Review*, CLXXX (September, 1905), 352–68. Satirizes Tarbell's history of the Standard Oil Company as premeditated myth-making.

NEVINS, ALLAN. Letter to the Editor. *American Historical Review*, L (April, 1945), 676–89. Replies to Destler's earlier article defending Lloyd against Nevins's charges of misrepresentation; documents his charges of Lloyd's unreliability as a historian of Standard Oil.

————. Review of Tarbell's *Life of Elbert H. Gary*. New York *World*, (November 25, 1925). Generally favorable, though Nevins notes disapprovingly her coolness toward labor unions.

STOLBERG, BENJAMIN. "St. Elbert of the Heavenly Trust." *The Nation*, CXXII (April 14, 1926), 414, 416. As the title implies, derides Tarbell's biography of Elbert H. Gary as mindlessly laudatory.

"TATTLER," "Ida M. Tarbell." *Nation*, CIV (January 18, 1917), 84. Contrasts Tarbell's personal charm and moderation with what the writer feels is her uncritical bias against tariff policies of big businessmen. Prefers the former.

THOMAS, BENJAMIN P. "Our Lincoln Heritage from Ida Tarbell."
Abraham Lincoln Quarterly, VI (March, 1950), 3–23. Credits
Tarbell for first interpretation of Lincoln as a typical pioneer
and for early contributions to the field of Lincoln studies. Considers her more as a Romanticist than as a Lincoln scholar.

TRAMBELL, CAROLINE T. "Ida Tarbell and Her Farm." *Country Life
in America,* XXIX (November, 1915), 19–22. Describes Tarbell's
home and her life as one of the early Connecticut exurbanities.

"Words From Women." Sunday feature in Lansing, Michigan, *State
Journal,* CXVI (July 19, 1970). The wife of California's Governor
Ronald Reagan, Nancy Reagan, comments adversely on the cur-
rent women's liberation movement.

Index